China
Connections

A Personal Journey

Ruth M. Lehtomäki

RAINBOW MEETS LAKE PUBLISHING
KEURUU
FINLAND

Rainbow Meets Lake Publishing
Kurkilahdentie 25
42700 Keuruu
Finland

www.rainbowmeetslake.net
ruth@rainbowmeetslake.net

Design and layout by SelfPublishing.com

Printed in the United States of America
RJ Communications LLC
51 East 42nd Street, Suite 1202
New York, NY 10017

ISBN 978-952-92-4253-5

This book is dedicated to

the three parents of the eight Fisher siblings

Harry Gladstone Fisher 1895–1960
Victoria Grace Fisher, née Bolton 1901–1941
Elsie May Fisher, née Thompson 1912–1990

Dad – this is for you, in loving memory.

For my five children –
words can never express my love for you all.

Also for my sisters
Ivy Paar, née Fisher 1933–1986,
who lived most of her adult life in Brittany, France,

and Dorothy Fisher 1932–1933,
who lived her short life in Lanping, China.

CHINA

—the very word floods me with mystery and longing. It is a far-off world that held my loved ones in her embrace and speaks to me of fathers and forgotten memories.

—My life has changed since you went away
And I need to know if I'm doing OK—

from 'Daddy Can You See Me?' by Anita Cochran

CONTENTS

Thoughts and Thanks

Five years ago, at the seasoned age of fifty-two, I started writing – two full-length autobiographical works, which have never been published due to their delicate, but explosive content. It was the pain and torment from my younger self that caused me to relive my life through the written word, and, in following that cathartic path, I discovered that I found writing easier than talking. In my first marriage, any voice I had was stifled and discredited, and in my second, well, I'm married to a Finn.

This book is an account of my personal journey through life in general and China in particular, and, as I no longer have any firm set of beliefs that would entitle me to be part of any labelled group, I will disappoint some members of my family who would have written this from the viewpoint of our Evangelical Christian upbringing. In all honesty to myself, I could not write from that perspective and trust that in following my heart, I will not offend or bring any form of suffering on another.

The timeline of events on any particular day has been construed from my memory and the perusal of sets of photos. For the first journey, that entailed two cameras set in different time zones, some six hours apart; for the second, a total of four clicking machines were involved, one set two hours later than the others and three that should have all registered the same time, but didn't. Any confusion or misrepresentation as to the order in which we woke, ate, walked, oohed and aahed, ate again, entered and exited vehicles and hotels, and so forth can be blamed on me.

I take full responsibility for the way in which the people mentioned in this book have been portrayed, as I could only write from my own position. Some names of people and places have been changed, but most are real.

Apologies to the Chinese for the Chinglish I have quoted, but I am not pointing out their interesting use of words and punctuation at the expense of any other country, including my own. English stallholders are renowned for their misuse of the apostrophe – anyone for apple's? – and Finglish abounds. Hopefully, American readers will not get confused with my British English, in which pants are trousers, and pantyhose are tights. You'll get your turn to feel at home somewhere in the middle of the book, when British readers will think I've forgotten how to spell.

As well as thanking all the family, friends, and organisations appearing in these pages, I owe a debt of gratitude to Marja-Leena Liljenmaa, who has encouraged and supported me from the first keystroke in 2003 to the present moment. I also want to thank her for unexpectedly making me a large copy of an old photo of my family from 1960 – before she realised that printing your own photos is an expensive hobby – which should now be hanging on a Chinese wall.

Special thanks go to Giles for being in the right place at the right time, to Ben for wanting to record our second trip, and to Thomas for designing and tending my website.

In China, my gratitude goes to Tien Yung, my Chinese pen pal, for his translations from Chinese to English – he had no hand in the Chinglish – and for his continued friendship. We will meet one day. Also thanks to the stallholder couple in Shanghai for their friendship.

Thanks are due for the following inclusions:

'Faith 3 – Home across the World' from *The Evening News* January 1945, quotes used by permission from The Evening News/Associated Newspapers Ltd.

'Valor: All for One' by John L. Frisbee from the December 1996 issue, reprinted by permission from *Air Force Magazine*, published by the Air Force Association.

'Missionaries in West China', from 'Papers of Joseph Francis Charles Rock, 1922–1962', quotes used with permission from © President and Fellows of Harvard College. Arnold Arboretum Archives.

To Plan Finland and Päivi Nepola in particular, thank you for allowing me to write about my sponsor visit, and to Plan China, especially Guo Lanlan, my gratitude for organising our trip so well. www.plan-international.org.

In the US, my thanks go to: Yvonne Kinkaid at the Air Force History Support Office at Bolling Air Force Base, Washington, D.C., for her assurance that the servicemen quoted in this book would have no objections; Gary Goldblatt of CBI Unit Lineages & History, for his advice and encouragement – www.cbi-history.com; Carl Weidenburner, for making history available online at http://cbi-theater.home.comcast.net; Len Fulton at Dustbooks, for responding so quickly to my mix-up; and Mike Stowe at www.accident-report.com.

Thank you to www.findmypast.com, www.genesreunited.co.uk, and www.friendsreunited.co.uk, for assisting me in my search for connections.

To my distant cousins, some through marriage, in the order I found you via the Internet – Dave Woods, Angela Woodhouse, Barbara Thorn, and Shirley Claridge. I extend my thanks to you all for helping me understand more of my Fisher heritage and for wanting to keep in touch. As you read this, it should mean that I have more time for incorporating all the information about our joint ancestry that you have passed on into my own findings.

To Eddie Brooks and Roger Clarke from junior school days,

who I re-found on *Friends Reunited* just before my second trip to China – thank you for helping me to re-evaluate my childhood.

Päivi Valkonen – thank you for helping me to articulate names, and to realise that the emotion of anger can sometimes be positive. Without your support a few years ago, I may never have found the courage to publish this book.

Thanks to Catrin Finch, the daughter of one of my college friends, for her inspiring harp playing, which accompanied me through many of the hours of writing – www.catrinfinch.com.

I would also like to thank Rod Quenby and Ulla Tulonen, who read through the text before it went for editorial scrutiny. Their suggestions proved invaluable and ironed out some discrepancies and possible confusion in both content and style.

Rod seems to be the proverbial jack-of-all-trades. In the past, he has even written a weekly column about nature and gardening in the British Isles. I trusted that such an occupation would help with words of a more international flavour and that he would find some of the instances where it might show that I have become more Finnish than English. For half the year I can easily say, 'It's minus today,' to any member of my family who might be listening, but I had forgotten that British and American readers would have no idea what I was talking about. He is also the husband of a woman who stood by me through difficult times and whose friendship has stood the test of time. Marion and I rarely see each other these days, but we can always pick up where we left off. Many thanks to her for sharing Rod's time.

Ulla had been retired for one year when I asked her to look at my text, following too many years teaching high school level English in my adopted hometown in Finland, which means she has taught the parents of many of the current students. I knew that she understood the intricacies of English grammar and punctuation from an EFL (English as a foreign language) perspective, whereas my understanding drifts with the wind. She explained the various uses of commas to me in an email, and finished by saying, 'I've mainly followed these principles, but you decide what to do because in literature there seem to be a lot of exceptions to these rules!' Since all this checking started, reading has become a headache for me as I stop and think, 'Well, I wouldn't have put a comma *there*.'

I would like to thank the following people who helped me through the last part of this journey, one which still continues. Lamar Cartwright and his son Alan, Dorothy Cereghino and her son Mark, Shelia Connor, Joseph Freda, Ken Joyce, Kent Keish, Townsell Marshall Sr. and Jr., Mrs Milton (Oscar's widow), John Newman, Ginger Staral, Khine Tun, Jay Vinyard, and Michael Woodhead.

If any relatives or friends of men who served in the China-Burma-India (CBI) arena of the Second World War think that they know someone who may have passed through my father's mission station or met him and his family in India on their way back to England, please contact me through my website, www. rainbowmeetslake.net with the name and any other information you have, and I will check in the notebook that he kept. If there's a match, I will scan you a copy of the entry – many are in the handwriting of the Americans themselves.

To all the people at SelfPublishing.com who helped me turn my dreams into a physical reality – a big thank you. With the aid of your website and the medium of email, you guided an absolute beginner through the maze of self-publishing barriers. I know I paid you for doing so, but you didn't have to be so patient and understanding as you were. So my thanks go to Jonathan Gullery, Carolyn Madison, Bob Powers, Ron Pramschufer, and other nameless individuals who handled my emails, payments, and queries. A special thank you goes to the editors for your corrections and suggestions.

And lastly, but by no means least, my love and gratitude go to Arto, who has allowed me to find myself.

Ja viimeisenä, muttei lainkaan vähäisimpänä, kiitollisuuteni ja rakkauteni Artolle, joka on antanut minun löytää itseni.

Ruth M. Lehtomäki
September 2008

Prologue

Spring 2006

'We'll have three weeks from work over Christmas and the New Year, so how about coming over then? Summer would be too hot, and, although spring and autumn are more pleasant weather-wise, you're all used to the cold and snow, aren't you?' Did I hear a subtle laugh in the background? 'Anyway, next summer we're planning a long trip, visiting you near the end before we return home, so that's out, isn't it?'

I checked flights on my computer, found a good offer, and pressed enter to finalize the payment. No turning back now unless I wanted to forfeit all that money, and, as I save rubber bands and bits of string for further use, I wasn't likely to do that.

Do you have a word or even a phrase from your childhood that elicits a tingle in your spine, or a fluttering in your midriff? It could be an object, a place, or someone's words, but whenever you hear, see, or catch a whiff of it, you are sent to an imaginary world that has nothing to do with your present reality. Grammatically, it may not warrant capitalising, but in your mind it has to be – there is no choice. No number of automatic checkers could force you to use insignificant small letters, although the passage of time might permit the use of only an initial capital.

What's yours? Charlie? Come Here *Now*? Kangaroos? Palms? Sunsets? Mine is CHINA, capitals all the way, and bold, italicised, and flashing if I dared, but this is my dream, and not even those little aids would be able to express what one small word can do to me – five little letters written in a particular order, spoken in a certain way, can turn my blood pale, make it shift through a spectrum of oranges until it reaches shades of yellow, oriental and mysterious. These days it is almost impossible to avoid my word, even supposing that's what I wanted to do. My family has a sponsored child in rural China, and we are constantly on the lookout for little presents that we can send her. What a task that is. It would have been much easier if we had chosen a child in Africa or Latin America. Many times I've gone into a shop and picked up a notepad and pencil from the counter, turned the packet in my hands, and read, 'Made in — ,' and thought, 'not this as well.'

Why my fascination with this word, when I have never visited the place or met more than a few of her people? How can this word fill me with longing and loathing, loss and pride, tastes, both sweet and bitter, when it is only a word?

To discover the answer to that, we need to go back more than a hundred and ten years to when a baby boy was born in Norfolk, England, to devout parents. Did they instil a love for foreigners in him? Were their methods of child rearing responsible for giving birth to his life's ambition? Was it a burning in his heart that gave him no rest? When did he first get the idea of travelling to the other side of the world to save the souls of one Asian race? I have no answers to those questions. I never asked.

'Daddy's gone to be with Jesus.' My mother spoke those words more than forty-five years ago, three months after my ninth birthday. I suppose I felt happy for my father, but I was jealous of my saviour who desired his company. Didn't I want him, too? My word took on a more sinister tone because I would no longer be able to make any discoveries about China directly from his lips, and until that time, I had had no thought that there was any kind of rush. Personal communication would no longer play a role in learning or attempting to understand what would make a man decide to leave his country. Where *did* he call home in the end? As his boat docked in Southampton, or wherever – I don't even know that detail, did his heart sing with homely feelings, or were those destined for when he arrived back in his mountainous village in the East? I have taken on his dilemma, if indeed he had one, of never knowing in which airport I am arriving home.

Harry Gladstone Fisher was born on 17 May 1895 into a world that is hard for me to imagine. As far as I know, there are no photos of him as a child and almost no snippets of what his childhood was like. The only things I gleaned from his twin sister, Bertha, many years after his death, were that he protected her at school from the bullies and that he went against his family's wishes when he embarked on his adventure to China. Whether she meant herself or her parents wasn't clear. He met his wife, a woman a few years his junior, while she was on furlough, having lived in China with her brother and his wife for several years. Soon after their marriage in September 1928, Harry and Victoria travelled together to China and established a home and church in a remote mountainous village in an area called Lanping, in the province of Yunnan, which means 'south of the clouds'. It is one of the most magnificent areas of that vast country according to all accounts. She gave birth six times between 1930 and 1941, and the last was too much for her. My father had already buried his second born, who had died in 1933, and he had to leave another beloved one behind him when war and circumstances forced his departure from the land he loved. He made the journey back to England – a man with no wife, no home, no job, very little money – and five children, aged between three and fourteen.

In January 1945, a few months after their escape, one edition of *The Evening News* had the headline, 'Faith, 3, Home – Across the world by mule, car, air and troopship' and contained the following information in the report.

—Mr. Fisher worked [in Lanping, Yunnan Province] for 16 years, seven days by mule track from any white neighbour, and there his children were born.—Mr. Fisher and his family were soon known to the Americans, who were especially grateful for his life-saving attention to a young officer suffering from infantile paralysis. In their gratitude, the Americans frequently dropped supplies to the lonely family, including shoes and sweets for the children—and four-penny bars of soap worth 10 s[hillings] in China. —[They] journeyed for days over rugged mountains on mules; then 100 miles by motor-car and truck; then 15 hours by American air transport; and from Bombay to Britain by troopship convoy.

Initially, they all lived together with Harry's eighty-one-year-old father, Samuel, in Orchard House, Hindolveston, Norfolk, and that is the address he still used in 1947 when his National Identity Card, number TSB 1804381, was stamped on 23 July. Even before that time, the children were cared for in different places and families as Harry endeavoured to make sense of his life. A lot of matchmaking ensued, but none of the Pentecostal candidates offered seemed right for him. He chose a Methodist lass from Yorkshire, a spinster-nurse of thirty-eight, seventeen years his junior. Elsie May was my mother. My love-hate affair with China had begun.

The only book I have which belonged to my father is a now-tatty A5-size hymn book, inscribed to *Mr H. G. Fisher* on board the *SS Carthage* on *23 May 1934* by *J. W. Bowman and family with deep gratitude for the friendship accorded.* After much investigation, I have discovered that this voyage was westwards, but I have been unable to ascertain where the ship sailed to and from. The book was published in Chicago three years earlier than the inscription, so presumably the giver was an American, but I can't be sure. The book I now treasure cost fifty cents, which included postage. Did Mr Bowman have a supply of hymn books for convivial fellow travellers, or do I have what was originally his personal possession, packed by his adoring wife or a servant? It's strange to think that the *SS Carthage* was launched in the same year as my keepsake was printed. My battered reminder of an unknown past has survived despite its flimsiness. Its twin did not fare as well, as demolition started eleven months after my father's decease. My internal longing for his return when there could be none reduced the ship, which had transported his breath from one side of the earth to the other, to scrap – parts and materials being recycled as my yearning for memories churned and catapulted in unison.

Since I was a child, I have wanted to visit China to try to capture some of the personal mystery of that word. I lived in South Korea for two years in the late 1980s without attempting to visit its westerly neighbour, not brave enough to traverse a country that had embraced a way of life completely different to the one in which I had been raised. It wasn't until the early part of the twenty-first century, when my second child was teaching in Sri Lanka and told me that his next abode would be in Shanghai, that a glimmer of light began to glow in my being. This would be my chance; someone I loved was back in the country that my father had treasured. He could be my guide and support to lay the ghosts to rest. Maybe my other children would share the journey, and we could all learn something about my father – their grandfather.

My second son and I created this adventure, and his wife and my three youngest children came along for the ride. My only regret on the journey was that my eldest son was unable to share it with us. His presence would have completed the magic. I trust that whether they accompanied me or not, all my children can discover a little about the blood that flows in their veins.

Chapter 1

Preparations

Packing and Presents

I seemed to have been packing for years: presents for family – little things added bit by bit to a Christmas carrier bag for Giles and Yoshi – different kinds of gifts for our Chinese sponsored child – a school bag filled item by item with useful and not so useful objects – and pieces of our clothing that wouldn't be needed before our departure. The folder with its many clear pockets had been receiving pieces of paper for months. E-tickets had been re-printed three times as plane schedules changed in ten minute increments. 'Good job they were cheap to start with,' I can remember thinking as the printer used another litre of ink, and the pile of copying paper diminished before my eyes. Their now defunct ancestors were left on a shelf for my husband, Arto, in our tiny office made from a walk-in closet, the new times altered by hand, so he could check our return date and time in our absence.

Visa forms had been filled in and sent to Helsinki. 'Please keep our passports safe on both journeys,' I silently asked as the packet was whisked to the back of the post office. As a non-Finn, mine had cost more than the children's. So much detail they had wanted, plus photos. How long will those sheets of paper be stored, I wonder? We had also had hepatitis shots, and, at fifty euros a go for each of us, plus the same pain and price in another few months, they were not cheap, but the twenty years' coverage should see me through whatever travelling I choose to do in the future. The children will need another dose if they get the wanderlust.

The biggest problem was guessing what clothes to take. By all accounts, we were going to face cold and snowy weather, not a problem for a woman who had just spent the last fourteen winters in Finland, and surely not for her three children who had only known such cold and darkness. Thomas had been born in South Korea, but was five months old when we came to live in my second husband's home country, nearing the end of winter, in 1991. I had been shocked to see ice everywhere at the beginning of April. Where were the spring flowers and green grass? These days I try not to ask, keeping such questions hidden in my heart. Spring appearing when summer should be arriving has become a way of life.

Thick coats and outer trousers, scarves, hats, and gloves all appeared on my lists, as well as winter boots and thick woollen socks to go inside them. As it turned out, much of it was never used, and, when it was, served no useful purpose. My own boots – bought at least one size too big to accommodate the aforementioned socks – proved unfit when I wore them all day around one of Beijing's huge indoor markets. As the weather was much milder than we had anticipated, I even refused to wear tights, and consequently the back of the boots rubbed the back of my legs raw. The marks they left were still in evidence six weeks later.

Rainwear and two umbrellas also found their way into our luggage, but along with the thick trousers, never saw the light of day. Even so, we still managed to only have three cases to check in at Tampere Airport, a large new backpack packed inside one of them, ready for cheap foreign goods. We had made the two-hour journey there from home in our car, Arto, as usual, acting as our chauffeur. Saturday, 16 December was a globally-warmed day. Finland had never known such a mild winter, up to that point at least, and there were strong indications that 'I'm Dreaming of a White Christmas' would need to be played incessantly on the radio. There had been little snow, and when it had deigned to show its presence, it had soon melted away with the non-seasonal temperatures. However, that morning had been freezing, and, although the sun was shining, I had to grab my husband's arm to avoid slipping as we left the car at the service station to go and have some lunch before our half-hour internal flight to Helsinki. He's quite used to my clinging onto him as my feet test the shiny surface and decide they need some support, my heart pounding with fear from ancient memories of trying to reach a hospital on foot, traversing icy pavements to have the wound on my face stitched up because the perpetrator wouldn't drive me, and there was no money for a taxi.

A short hop later, we were in the capital's main airport, which is still minute compared to those of other countries. Christmas was in the air, and so were the Chinese as we realised that our flight would serve as acclimatisation for our next three weeks in a foreign culture.

The small screens hanging from the overhead storage compartments in the plane slowly made the countdown of our 7,400-kilometre journey. There had been many things to plan and organise over the previous five months, and my mind was reeling. 'Are you really on a plane,' I asked myself as the children tried to find suitable music on their headphones, 'that is going to take you to China? Are you actually doing this? Are you sure you haven't gone raving mad, Ruth?'

Chapter 2

Shanghai

Family and Dance

Seventeen hours after leaving home, we arrived on China's shores, eight o'clock on Sunday morning for Shanghai, two o'clock for us. None of us had slept very much, although we had tried. One movie after another had filled the screens, none of which seemed to be in just the right position for my eyes. The food had been good, and as usual, I had put unused sugar bags and refresher wipes into my bag. Waste, I cannot.

Immigration took an age, almost as long as it had taken to fill in the three forms times four that had been passed to us on the plane. Did they honestly think we were going to tick 'yes' to a question relating to bringing arms into the country, or on the health form, that anyone would admit to having a contagious disease? Each form was collected at different points on our trip from plane to airport exit, and I wondered who was going to read them and how long they would be in storage.

Eventually, we emerged into the receiving area and saw a tired-looking face belonging to Giles. Ours were not any more alive, but we greeted each other with smiles and hugs – the beginning of an adventure many months in the making. With Thomas pushing our laden trolley as best he could, Giles directed us towards the latest in railways, the first commercial high-speed magnetic levitation line in the world. I have heard that they are expensive to construct and not cost effective to run, so in future, maybe they will only be installed in places with money to burn. Construction had begun in March 2001, and it was opened to the public on New Year's Day, by the solar calendar, 2004. The train can reach a speed of 350 km/h in two minutes, with a maximum of 431 for normal situations. We have a personal photo showing 416. Shanghai scenery whizzed past us as we made our way to Long Yang Road Station on Subway Line 2, about thirty kilometres away. During the seven-minute-and-twenty-second journey, we tried to locate ourselves in space and time.

· ᘒ ᖾ

The block of flats towered above us as we emptied out of the taxis and made our way to the huge glass doors, pulling and carrying our luggage with us. The lift was airing adverts on a small television screen, but we had little time to watch them as we were soon on the twentieth floor and entering a modern, spacious flat containing a blue-and-silver-decorated Christmas tree in the living room. This space had been home to my son Giles and his Sri Lankan wife, Yoshi, for the last eighteen months. They had both been living in her country at the time of the 2004 tsunami and had made many relief trips to the worst-hit areas with food and medicine using their own money and some raised by family and friends. Later they distributed school bags and equipment for the children who had suddenly found themselves with nothing. They were now living their travel dream. As a maths teacher, Giles could find work anywhere in the world, I imagine. His choice of Shanghai had enabled my dreams to breathe.

Yoshi is a famous dancer in her country and had run her own dancing school there. She began ballet training at the age of five and, during her teens, was trained in jazz and contemporary techniques. That early foundation had opened the door to her future as she undertook twenty-eight years of international competition-level training in many kinds of dance. In 2001, she won the SE Asia Latin American crown in Singapore. She had continued her passion in her new city, the largest in China with a population of over eighteen million – 2,804 people to every square kilometre, give or take a few, as compared to under twenty in Finland. No wonder it's so silent in my adopted country. It was hard to imagine, looking down and across from the balcony, that only ten years before, much of the land that now held various styles of modern housing had been rice paddies.

During the autumn, Yoshi had been putting a children's dance show together. They were mainly foreign children, the sons and daughters of expats, most of whom were attending Giles's school. Some were Chinese – from the rich end of society – a contrast to what we would see only four days later.

The flat was quiet, but not exactly empty, when we arrived. Yoshi was already at school preparing for the first night's performance, but a former student from Colombo still lay asleep in the guest room. She slept through the tumult of us parking our cases in the master bedroom and trying to decide what day and time it was and where on earth we were. It is an emotional experience for me to be in the physical presence of my two eldest sons, and this was no exception, but I was determined not to cry about actions taken in the past that could never be reversed. 'Act naturally,' I told myself, but whoever does that? Is anybody living the way their inner heart knows is true? Do people act their way through life, changing characters and roles as they mingle with different people?

Jet lag overcame the three younger ones, and before long, they were all lying side by side on top of Giles and Yoshi's bed – fortunately king size. The living room was full of boxes containing the evening's programmes, but not in a form ready for handing out, so when the children awoke from their unscheduled sleep, we spent the next few hours fitting and stapling them together, and realising how much effort Yoshi had put into this event. She would need the holiday that we were going to spend together, as would Giles. He would be working until just before we left Shanghai, although at the time, I didn't understand just how close.

We visited Giles's school and saw his classroom and also Yoshi amidst her preparations. It was a new building in a traditional English style, built on rented land that the local authorities can reclaim at any time. Precarious might be a suitable word to describe the situation. Being a franchise of a famous British institution, it became the best school in Shanghai before the foundations had been laid. Now that it's up and running, its uniqueness has won the love of the Chinese. Lunch – or was it breakfast, or even dinner? – was at a Japanese-style sushi bar where the small plates of various victuals passed by on a narrow conveyor belt. It felt like being in a factory belonging to a doll's house. The bill was calculated from the number of empty plates at your departure. The food was delicious, and so were the prices; we couldn't believe it.

The show in the evening was an entrancing experience. The children, who Yoshi told us had been practising hard for months, put all their efforts into moving to the music. Jumi, the visiting artiste, danced like a professional, her moves exciting and enticing. Different tempos and styles of dance filled the auditorium, but maybe the boys received the loudest applause – for their bravery. The mistakes that Yoshi knew had occurred through the evening's performance went unnoticed by me and by most of the rest of the audience, I imagine. Tamara, my youngest at twelve, and I decided to return the following evening. Thomas and Timo, sixteen and thirteen, declined. Once was more than enough.

On Monday morning, after Giles had gone to school, the four of us girls went on a shopping trip. We left the two boys

sleeping and found them in the same state when we returned
several hours later. Yoshi used the intercom to contact one of
the guards on the gate to order a taxi. It left the compound, and
Tamara and I watched the passing world. There were many skyscrapers of various shapes, one group looking like silver lipstick
tubes, and lots of traffic. Palm trees, a surprise, were tied up for
the winter, their trunks looking like giant sisal vases. Everything
looked new and modern when, without warning, we turned into
a narrow, shantytown street with small, unkempt stalls lining it
on each side. Pedestrians ruled this part of the city, and the horn
was in constant use. Emerging on the other side, we came to a
wide street populated with people in modern, expensive fash-
ions. It was like waking from a dream. The driver's short cut had
shown us the realities.

I couldn't believe how cheap the ride had been, but the value
of money soon lost all meaning as I converted yuan to euros.
Who was kidding whom? The market was huge, on many levels,
and packed with tiny stalls manned mainly by young women. As
we passed, they would emerge from their overloaded spaces and
shout 'Hello', 'Watches', 'Scarves' … We only had to glance at
some item that might be of interest, and the shopkeepers were
on us like hawks on the hunt. I rarely need help when shopping
– I'm just looking, thank you – but here I encountered persist-
ence to a degree I had not experienced before. Was it necessity?
How much could each person make a week with so many people
offering the same kinds of goods?

Jumi had to collect some silk clothes that she had been meas-
ured for, and even though this had been planned as a surveying
trip for Tamara and me, when I saw the stunning materials and
styles, I decided to be taped for a coat. I chose a plain black
silk material, but when the shopkeeper told me that the gar-
ment could be reversible, I added a peacock blue. Before leaving
home, I had thought that I would like to find a Chinese-style
jacket with a modern twist. Here it was, and at about fifteen

euros each, why not choose two more colours, with a different neckline?

Our Sri Lankan visitor was thinking of buying a bag, but none of the ones that the stallholders produced in the cubicle we eventually entered after much hunting were suitable. Before I had time to blink, she had disappeared into a space at the side of the stall that had been concealed by shelves full of bags. One of the stallholders had slid the shelves outwards and across and then pushed them back into place. I had the eerie feeling that Jumi was being kidnapped, although this was clearly not the case. She still didn't find what she was looking for among the presumed illegal knock-offs in the huge cave-like expanse of further storage facilities.

We passed some common stalls with out-of-the-ordinary names, such as a bookshop called *England bridge*, the name printed in red over a photograph of Tower Bridge. On the *Escalator notice Board* was the sentence, *The child must have the adult care*. It further informed us that we were in the Shanghai South Bund Soft-Spinning Material Market. That would be good to know if you got lost and needed to let someone know where you were – if you could remember such a mouthful. We bought some covers for wine bottles and tissue-boxes, and various small, embroidered items to give as gifts from one small hole-in-the-wall, which advertised the fact that it sold: *Tablecloth cushion for leaning on, napkin paper box*. Maybe singular and plural are different concepts in Shanghai's language.

In the afternoon, as we were walking along the pavement towards a metro station, an elderly woman accosted me, and pointing to my bag held out her hand. Yoshi grabbed my other arm and pulled me away but the woman followed, her grip tightening on my upper arm until it hurt. I thought about giving her something just to avoid the unpleasantness, but I realised at the same time that there might be other people in the area who would immediately join us. I felt very vulnerable and I hoped that other visitors were not subjected to the same routine.

We returned to the shopping centre near Giles's school and saw our only tai-chi practitioner of the trip, although at the time, I had been expecting to see some in Beijing in the coming days. The middle-aged woman was alone in a quadrangle, visible to everyone who was walking through the glass mall, and she seemed peaceful and relaxed. I would gladly have watched her for much longer than I had time for.

The second performance that evening was equally well attended, and Tamara and I were able to help with the clearing up of props and equipment afterwards. Giles and Yoshi had organised a buffet meal for the performers at an Irish pub, owned, surprisingly enough, by an Irishman and his Chinese wife, the latter a necessity for such a venture. Giles returned home with their personal equipment and picked up Thomas and Timo. After their arrival at the restaurant, we ordered a meal each, something we rarely do, but did many times in the following weeks. We celebrated Yoshi's achievements with her, Giles, and two other teachers from Giles's school, who had become their best friends in China. I couldn't have chosen a better way to spend the final night of the first part of our stay in Shanghai.

Chapter 3

Xian

Sponsorship and Protection

The overnight train took seventeen hours to travel the 1,600 kilometres from Shanghai to Xian and cost about fifty euros each, a measly sum when compared to Finnish prices. The compartments had four bunk beds each, and I was glad that I didn't have to clamber up to one of the top ones. The morning had been busy with Jumi, with Yoshi's help, ramming her accumulated souvenirs into her case and leaving for home; Yoshi and us packing for a trip around China; and Giles teaching at school. The day before, he had given us a deadline for leaving the flat, but as he arrived home from work later than he had anticipated, it passed. However, we still made it to the train on time. Yoshi had received several bouquets of flowers the evening before, and I felt sad that we couldn't take them with us to give to the people we would be meeting in Xian, but our hands were already full of luggage.

Giles and Yoshi would be sleeping in the next cubicle, which they discovered they would be sharing with two Chinese men, so they spent the evening with us, ordering food from the train buffet, playing cards, reading, and chatting. The days since our arrival had been hectic, and we had all been rushing around in different directions, but now the six of us were cooped up in a rabbit hutch. When Giles and Yoshi decided to go to their chamber and retire for the night, I noticed that Giles tucked his small backpack under our bunks. 'Better safe than sorry,' passed through my mind as I guessed that their passports and money, as well as all the plane tickets for our domestic flights, were inside.

Sleep eluded me as we rattled through the Chinese land-scape, bright lights appearing and disappearing through the curtains like flashes of lightning. It seemed a shame that we hadn't been able to make this trip during daylight, I thought as I wondered what kinds of landscape and civilisation we were passing. Morning was a relief as the staff bustled up and down, emptying bins and stripping beds.

The day that had been in the planning for many months, and which had eventually been chosen as Tuesday, 20 December, had finally arrived. As we joined the mass exodus from Xian station, it was hard to take in that we were in the city that was famous for its Terracotta Army – and the area of China where our Plan-sponsored child lived.

Plan was founded by a British journalist, John Langdon-Davies, and a refugee worker, Eric Muggeridge, in 1937, to provide basic necessities for children whose lives had been transformed by the Spanish Civil War. Later, this included more of Europe as the Second World War took its toll on the lives of children. As Europe recovered, it became apparent that other countries were also in need of assistance, so in the 1950s, Plan started working with deprived children in Africa, Asia, Latin America, and the Caribbean and renamed itself Plan International.

More than fifty years later, it is one of the largest development organisations in the world, working in forty-nine developing countries in the areas of health and housing, education and live-lihood, and water and sanitation. The foundation of their work is child sponsorship, with one million sponsors in seventeen countries helping the same number of children and their families all over the world.

Our sponsored child, let's call her Caidie, had been a few months short of her sixth birthday when we started our monthly sponsorship payments. She was now ten, and we had watched her grow through the photographs that the Plan office in Helsinki periodically sent us. I had chosen her country because my father had made the same choice. We had been told that she lived with her parents and grandparents in a remote rural village, depending on the land for sustenance. One outside hole in the ground served as a toilet for the entire community. The school roof leaked, and life consisted mainly of surviving. Our money helped remedy some of the problems. I hoped that if people had lived in such a situation all their lives, they would be happy. How much of an individual's unhappiness, after all, is connected to what they think they need or want? I still wanted to be a small part of improving their living conditions and bringing a little unexpected joy into Caidie's life through my letters, photos, and small gifts.

It had taken many emails between Helsinki, Shanghai, Xian, and me to organise this day, but I knew it had all been worth it when I saw the placard held high above the waiting heads. Underneath was our driver for the day. He was glad to see us, but we soon realised that there would be no verbal communication between us apart from the basic words that Giles and Yoshi had learned. We walked to the minibus with our luggage, and, thinking that we were going straight to Caidie's village, I wondered how we were going to make ourselves understood or learn anything about her life. The drive took us beyond the borders of the city until we were heading north on an empty dual carriageway. The road was new, but underused, and I imagined it was preparation for a bright future of commerce.

The local area office with its English-speaking staff was a pleasant surprise after a two-hour journey. It was cold inside, and they were wearing their coats at their desks. I knew their Finnish counterparts would not be wearing theirs. We were offered hot water, a drink I have never liked, but it was warming, and this was not the kind of situation in which you could refuse. Needing the toilet before we commenced the second part of our trip, we were told it was on the next floor. This was our first encounter with the Chinese version of that amenity, and our noses noticed first. The camera and camcorder were put to use as the children recorded this momentous event of seeing a hole in the floor surrounded by a ceramic foot stand. I told them about an article I had found before our departure on a web page about China. When Beijing first introduced western-style toilets to its public sanitary system, cleaners often found shoeprints on the seats. We strained to imagine people perched on the tops of western toilets, trying to keep their balance and perform.

The two young lady interpreters joined us in our bus, and four male members of the staff sped off in front of us in another. It was past noon by now, and we passed a town school dismissing its pupils for lunchtime. No school meals provided in this place, it seemed. The traffic wove in and out, and pedestrians crossed the road wherever and whenever they wanted. Before long we were into countryside and bumping our way over a narrow dirt track that wound between barren fields and orchards. I tried to imagine this ride in the summer with the crops growing and the trees in bloom. It would look much brighter and more optimistic, but the heat would be unbearable.

Buildings came into view, and the bouncing lessened, for which our backsides were thankful. One-storey houses lined the street with large piles of dried vegetation in front of some and stacks of bricks in front of others; everything seeming to be in the middle of some operation. When the minibus stopped in front of an open doorway, we decided that we must have arrived. The two vehicles quickly emptied, and we looked around us. I attempted to adjust to this scene, standing outside the house that Caidie called home. I expected her to come out and greet us, but it was her grandfather who did that, a shy smile on his face. Were we the first foreigners this village had seen? It seemed rude to ask.

We were ushered inside, directly into a large, barren room. A shaft of sunlight shone through a hole at the top of one wall just below the rafters, splitting the room and forcing the dust mites to dance in its warmth. There was no ceiling attached to the cross beams, so the open space under the lining of the roof was used as storage for various wooden items. A pair of cats, both scrawny-looking, peered at us from behind an old iron pot that had a frying pan on top. Two square tables pushed together with differing plastic cloths – one patterned red, the other blue – were laden with plates of sweets, peanuts, and seeds. We were asked to sit around on chairs and stools, and later I realised that some of these must have come from neighbours as they poured through the door to view the spectacle. It felt as though we were the proverbial monkeys in a cage, but I thought a proficient breeder like a rabbit would have been a more appropriate metaphor when the women, some of the younger ones holding toddlers in their arms, all laughed at me after the Plan staff told them that I was the mother of four of the young people with me. I chose not to mention the absent fifth, not wanting to overemphasise the difference between our lives as mothers. I hope that they can still laugh about our visit and that we brought some sunshine into their lives, if only for a few hours.

The tea was hot, and the nuts tasted good. We put our empty shells on the corner of the table; the Plan workers and locals put theirs on the rough, dirt floor. Maybe each culture in the room was thinking how barbaric the other was. There had still been no sign of the child of the family, but we were told she was on her way, her father having gone to the school to collect her.

A timid, red-coated girl appeared at the door, clinging to her father and apparently unable to believe there were such a lot of people in her home. She was almost pushed towards me and sat down, bewilderment and confusion written on her beautiful face. She never let a smile find its way to the surface, but I hope that the memory of that day has allowed her to since. I gave her a birthday present for a month previously. Other years, they had gone through the Plan postal system, but knowing that we would see her, I had kept it to give to her personally. It was a pink hat and gloves, made in Finland, and a scarf that I had knitted for her. The hat was a good fit, but her hands will have to grow somewhat to make use of the gloves. I hope that no one else decides to use them meanwhile, as one of the women found the scarf irresistible and had it round her neck almost before it was out of the packet.

The blue school bag was next. I showed her some of the things, collected for months after checking the 'Made in — ' labels, those that had ended in 'China', having been removed from their packaging. She took some interest, but was still concerned by all the eyes on her. I tried not to add to the confusion, but wanted her to know that she meant a lot to me and that I had her photo in my living room. What that cute little remark meant to her, I never considered at the time, failing to link the bare, unplastered walls and lack of furniture with anything as frivolous as a photo frame.

I had brought a scarf with me for the grandmother, and I took it to her at the back of the house – a dark and dreary area where she had been cooking. We were the same age, but I felt much younger as I saw the signs of a hard life on her face. I held her hand, and it was like stroking tree bark. She was all smiles, which made up for her granddaughter's lack of them, and she immediately put the scarf around her neck over the coat she needed to wear, even when preparing food. Looking now at the photo of her and me together, smiles covering our faces, top teeth on view, I notice that hers are much whiter than mine – a reward for her simple life in the Chinese countryside – unless of course, they are false.

The sun was still shining as we were ushered out of the house and stood in the courtyard with the family and neighbours. Greenhouse gases had followed us from the west it seemed. Meanwhile the grandmother was clearing the snacks and replacing them with hot food, including bean sprouts, tofu, vegetables, and plates of steamed, pure-white rolls. Chopsticks waited at each place and beckoned us to join them. I felt bad about eating this family's food, especially when we were told that this was a feast; their normal food was much simpler and of smaller quantities. Someone showed us how to split the roll and add what we wanted from any of the dishes. As this method of eating got underway, we were each served with a bowl of hot noodles. Such generosity was all too much for me, and I found it hard to swallow the delicious food. Everyone else was tucking in, and I hoped that the family itself would enjoy the food later and remember it as a special day.

I saw the grandmother coming towards me clutching the gift bag that had held my present, now bulging with material. 'Oh no,' I thought, 'she's going to give me something. This is not why I came here. I have so much.'

In the corner of the room was an old wooden loom, similar to ones I have seen in some homes in Finland, only shabbier and clearly homemade. In a split second, I knew that she was bringing me some of her work. Had she made it for her family to use or to sell? Both scenarios filled me with dread. How could I serenely refuse such a gift without giving offence? I had come to give, not to receive. With one of the translators in tow, she handed me the package and started to explain that the white, natural piece of material was for kitchen use, and the large green and maroon item was a bedspread. Tears were in my eyes as I tried to tell her that I was grateful, but she had to keep them. She was insistent. All I could do was hug her and stroke the work-hardened hands that had spent hours to produce what was now mine. Little did she guess that what she saw as suitable for dishcloths, I saw as an attractive table runner or curtain.

⚬∽⚬

Through one of the translators, we learned from the village leader about the new roof that Plan had built on the school and the single outside toilet that had replaced the hole in the ground. He walked with pride as he led us through another building to a piece of land that was backing on to the fields. The walls of the public convenience were rough brick, and there was no door, although the squatting-style toilet was out of view. Chickens pecked around, and a goat sprang into a winter-weary bush to get out of our way. Whether these were communal livestock or belonged to one family in particular, we never ascertained.

As we were walking along one of the dusty streets towards the school, I picked up some of the dried material that we had seen piles of and saw that some of them were cotton husks, some of which perhaps had supplied the thread that grand-mother had used for the weaving that was now tucked into my luggage. The sunshine had brought some elderly women into the street to play mah-jong, the colourful tiles almost covering the small table on to which they were throwing crumpled notes. Giles, the mathematician, studied their play intently. We were ushered on; otherwise he might be an expert by now. Entering a gateway, we saw the school in front of us and heard singing issuing from the doorways.

The bleak room was full of children sitting at old wooden tables, a few piles of books on some of them. One small girl in the middle was singing in phrases, and then everyone else copied her, parrot-fashion. Whether this was for our benefit, or it was a regular lesson, no one explained. The teacher was a middle-aged man who stood at the front and let it continue. I wasn't sure what we should do, apart from stand and listen until one of the young women with us said that was enough, and we started clapping. Here there were some smiles, but these children didn't have the pressure of everyone's attention solely on them. We gave out some stickers, other small presents, and also a jigsaw map of Finland. The postcards of our hometown were meant for the teacher to display, but they were hastily distributed – there was nothing on the walls for them to join anyway. An old man and two small children sat by the open door at the back of the room, wearing coats, as were most of the children. We were told later that trained teachers do not want to come to these small rural communities, so more often than not, it is a villager who takes on the role. As we walked away and admired the new roof, I couldn't help thinking of the children I had seen in the school in Shanghai, and Giles's classroom, its walls covered in posters posing interesting questions for the pupils, stimulation surrounding them as they studied.

A large majority of China's rural population relies upon agriculture as its primary source of livelihood, but erosion, contamination from pesticides, and poor farming techniques have led to low crop productivity. Poor access to health care and education are also problems facing China's population. In rural areas, Plan's main objective is to provide resources and expertise, enabling communities to control their own development. China's economy continues to grow, but as in the past, most of this growth occurs in urban areas, while the majority of rural families still live in poverty. During 2006, Plan was able to support 18,300 children and their communities in these situations.

Our Caidie is one of those.

Before returning to Xian, we were taken to an Emperor's burial area; a long road lined with statues led to a mountain where the royal personage had been buried. We were told the history of the place, but I'm afraid the details never registered in my brain. Back at the local office, I gave the man who seemed

to be the boss a photo book about Finland in Chinese. I had
been so pleased when I had found it in a bookstore several
months before our departure. We were asked to fill in a report
sheet about our visit, and Giles gave them his contact details,
wondering whether he could support them in some way with a
group of volunteers from his school.

   Driving back to the city in the late afternoon, thinking about
Caidie and her life, my thoughts turned to my own childhood.
My days in primary school had been strange. Not only was I the
only 'born-again' Christian in my class, but also the one who
had some connection with a land far away. The only trouble
was that there *was* no link for me. I had been born in England
and had only heard stories, which, after my father's death, took
on a life of their own in my imagination. One day, I remember
taking the Lord's Prayer to school. Nothing odd in that you
say, after all, every day started with assembly and hymn singing
– 'All things bright and beautiful' – and prayers, but why did
the headmaster have to read them? In my church, people stood
up and spoke their own words. This frail piece of paper held
squiggles and marks that no one had seen before. The Chinese
characters filled the browning sheet and shrieked that I was a
freak. I felt that my fellow schoolmates were pondering, 'who
is she?' – but that might have all been in my head too. I know
that in my heart, I blamed my mother who had told me to take
it in to show my teacher. In high school, during my oral test for
O level French, my teacher, Miss Baker, asked me a question
with 'la Chine' in it. I didn't know that word and kept asking
her to repeat it. Finally, she had to tell me, in English, that it
meant China, and she was asking me about being born there.
As I hadn't been, the query had made no sense to me at all. I
did pass the exam, but only just, I imagine. How did *she* know
of my China connection?

Xian was dark when we returned. We drove through many back streets before finally stopping outside a tall building, the hotel that Giles had pre-booked for us. I left some Finnish sweets and a small book on the front seat for the driver and tried to pay him for the petrol we had used, but he refused to take it. Among other things, the Plan literature about sponsors' visits had stated that we were responsible for this expense. Neither of us had any language with which to resolve the issue, but he left quickly before I could force some notes between his clenched fingers.

The reception area where we walked with our luggage was expansive and adorned with a huge decorated Christmas tree; two miniature versions stood on the desk. We only needed rooms for one night, and after Giles viewed the ones available, we ascended in the lift, and the children and I discovered a large room with two single beds designed for giants. The boys shared one, and Tamara and I the other. It was a neat arrangement. The shower was hot, and the toilet was raised and had a seat, a vast difference from the way of life we had experienced that day. It was hard to believe that we were only a few hours' drive away from a small hut that served a whole village. Did the people living in this city, and those we had rubbed shoulders with in Shanghai, have any idea how the majority of their fellow citizens were living? How many of them were sponsors for a child in their own country?

We ventured out into the lights of the city, the ancient buildings lit against the night sky. Enchanting and bewitching, the scene was spoilt by some glowing yellow arches, emphasizing again the spread of less-desirable western influences. It was at this point I told the children that we would not be entering one of those establishments during our trip, but an hour later we were in a Pizza Hut. As we sat there being served by young people wearing red outfits to fit the time of year, I couldn't keep my thoughts from returning to Caidie and her life.

There is no lack of money in this world, although there seems to be some confusion about how it should be used. My whole life, I have felt myself to be on the edge of society, with just sufficient funds to get me by. This is also true in my adopted country, where I will receive not much more than the minimum pension in fewer years than I care to admit.

Later that evening, lying in bed with the noises of a Xian night pulsing around me, I had never felt so rich. Compared to Caidie I was a millionaire – or more. Never again would I think of asking my husband to install a second toilet in our two-storey house. One between five of us seemed almost a luxury. Why should I complain when a rural community had one – outside – between them? As I made my way towards a clean, flushing receptacle, I wondered if someone was trudging through the dark right now to make use of the one we had seen earlier that day. Or was there a bucket in the corner of the room for that purpose? I had so many unanswered questions.

Hot orange juice, another first, awaited us at the buffet breakfast. As this was included in the price of the room, I wanted to eat, but breakfast and I are not the closest of friends. Coffee was available on request, and, as I drank mine, I watched, fascinated, as my companions ate their choice of food with chopsticks. I took the opportunity to read the *For Your Information* printed on the tiny packet that held our key card, where I found the following: *Please return keycard to the front desk upon out or check-out. It should be paid for the damage or lose the keycard.*

After our repast, we stored our luggage in Giles and Yoshi's room as we would be checking out in the evening after our day's excursion. I couldn't stop myself taking a photo of a round, red metal object that was mounted on the corridor wall near our rooms that declared itself to be a *Hydr Ant*. It did make me wonder what kind of insects I might encounter during our trip.

Descending in the lift and exiting the hotel, we were all eager to find the warriors.

The Terracotta Warriors and Horses were the most significant archaeological excavations of the last century. Work is ongoing at this site, which is around 1.5 kilometres east of Emperor Qin Shi Huang's Mausoleum. When he ascended the throne in 246 BC at the age of thirteen, Qin Shi Huang, later the first Emperor of all China, began work on his last resting place, which took eleven years to finish. In recent times, there had been speculation that buried treasures and sacrificial objects had accompanied the emperor into his afterlife. In 1974, the year my first child was born, a group of farmers discovered some pottery while digging for a well near the royal grave. Archaeologists went to Xian to study the finds and to make further excavations. They recognised that these artefacts were associated with the Qin Dynasty (211–206 BC).

The following year, a museum was built on the site, and since then, it has become a must-see on tourists' lists, including the Chinese themselves. During our visit, there were more native than foreign visitors. The area covers 16,300 square metres and includes three pits; Pit No. 1 being the first discovered. Naturally.

We had arrived at the site by taxi, two to be correct, three boys and girls to each. The drivers must have been in cohorts because both vehicles arrived at a spa, and refused to take us to the warriors. Maybe the business paid them a commission. A couple of months after our return home, we watched an episode of the American show, *Amazing Race*, in which the competing couples had to get themselves to the warriors. One duo experienced the same problem we had and landed up in a different place. They expressed their frustration rather differently and with much more feeling than we did, but then we didn't have a vast number of dollars at stake, and getting angry wouldn't have changed our situation. We found another pair of vehicles and finally arrived at our destination. The entrance was miles from the buildings themselves, so we needed to walk along a wide path that was lined with new shop buildings, few of them occupied. 'Will the rest be manned by the time of the Olympics in nineteen months' time?' I wondered. Building and planting was ongoing, and I imagined that in spring and summer, it would look picturesque.

As we continued our stroll, we were stopped several times by people trying to sell us souvenirs. One little boy of about ten years of age with a scarred face tried to sell me a pack of picture postcards. My heart went out to him, but my hand didn't go out to my purse. He ran off to the next opportunity.

Having bought our tickets and put the entrance barriers behind us, we emerged into a vast courtyard and started with the museum. It wasn't especially exciting, but there were some interesting photos of the Clintons surrounded by clay soldiers; were they anticipating a similar final resting place? I picked up a leaflet in there and studied the map of the entire area showing the whereabouts of all the buildings housing the soldiers, the toilet blocks, the clinic, and the cinema. I was intrigued when I noticed a blue dot on a path next to the symbols for left luggage, police, and way out, surrounded by green shapes depicting grass. I checked the key and found that the blue circle meant, 'You are here'. Whoever had decided to put that piece of information on a mobile map must have had an interesting sense of humour.

Sensing the children's boredom, we re-emerged into the cool, winter's day. We entered one of the pits, which was dark and dank, and I was surprised at how few soldiers there were. Where were they? This was nothing like the photos I had seen, and disappointment spread through my being. We were walking above excavation works, which, without expectations, would have been impressive. How much do people miss in life because they are hoping for much more, failing to see the wonder and mystery that surrounds them at the present moment?

The next building was also in some way a letdown. Life-size terracotta figures of soldiers and horses arranged in groups met our eyes, and I began to feel some of the mystery of the place, but it still wasn't as vast as I had imagined, and I thought the pictures I had seen must have been fakes. Maybe we should have started with Pit No. 1, but sometimes it's best to keep the best until last.

Pit No. 1 is oblong, 230 metres east to west, and 62 metres north to south. This is what I had been waiting for – row upon row of life-size warriors in different states of readiness, more than 6,000 of them standing in battle formation. One puff of magic dust, and they would have started moving towards me.

Tamara and I ventured to the toilet block, dreading what we might find, but surprise, surprise, lemon-scented air accosted our nostrils, and the western, pure-white loos were spotlessly clean. We could have stayed there longer, as tourists, admiring the sparkle and smells, but the others were waiting, and it was chilly outside. Spying a café that looked as though it had only recently opened, we ventured in, and as the only customers, were warmed up immediately with hot drinks.

On our way towards the main exit and the taxis, we all bought varying-sized clay figures of warriors and horses, some for personal use, others to give away as presents. This had been accomplished after much haggling and moving from stall to stall. As we walked along carrying our purchases, the little boy with scars on his face approached me again. He was offering me a pack of postcards. I had already bought some, but my heart had remained with him, and I gave him double the asking price, instead of half – or less – which would be usual. As he ran off, I understood that he was more than likely being used as bait, and when a short walk later I saw him beside a small wooden stall with a woman who was the right age to be his mother, my fears were heightened. Had I fallen into the trap that another human being had set for me? Had he deliberately been scarred to attract my sympathy, and did he know that fact? The over-payment had been nothing to me in monetary terms, but had it cost him his dignity?

When we returned to Xian, we wandered the back streets and found one with a large banner draped across its entrance: Welcome to Beijuan men Islamic street. As we saw many women also selling their wares, I can only imagine that the word *men* was a mistake or should have been attached to *Beijuan*. We were instantly in another world of foreign facial features, clothes, smells, and food, which seemed to transport us out of China and into the Middle East. Foreigners equal money, and we were accosted and cajoled and irritated. The choice and tightness of the stalls was stifling, and once we had shown interest in some item, other stallholders would join in the haggling. It was an exhausting experience, but I made some purchases and hoped I had helped to put more than just food on their tables. Wandering back on to the modern main shopping street, we found a small restaurant, which was rather western-looking, but on further scrutiny, we realised it was a Chinese chain. We all tried different items from the menu, and Timo, much to our surprise, was served a plate piled high with waffles and cream. I had my doubts as to whether he could eat it all, but I shouldn't have had. From that experience, I learned not to trust the translations on menus, or at least my interpretation of them.

As we emerged from the café, my eye was caught by a large message hung on the side of a building wishing us all, in true Chinese fashion, a *MEYRRC HRISTMAS*. I had to take another photo.

Chapter 4

Beijing

Christmas and Tourism

We boarded another overnight train, which again cost about fifty euros each, but this time we would only be travelling for twelve hours. 'Be grateful for small mercies,' came to my mind. The compartments were more luxurious than in the first train we had travelled on, but the environment was still not conducive to sleep. Two taxis had dropped us at Xian station after we had collected our luggage from the hotel, following our trip to the warriors. As Yoshi, Tamara, and I emerged from our vehicle, the world was dark and disorientating. Our luggage was in the closed boot, and the driver didn't seem in any hurry to open it and remove the bags for us; he remained stuck to his seat. Fearing that he might drive off with our belongings, intentionally or not – my thoughts weren't all black – I banged on the boot lid to get his attention in the midst of the cacophony of the station forecourt. As no click clicked or door opened, I banged again. That annoyed him, and he got out and started shouting at me; very customer-friendly behaviour. My heart was racing, not only because of the current shouting, but with memories of more personal words that had been flung at me in a language I understood. However, he eventually opened the boot, but he didn't help us retrieve our luggage. Still shaking, I walked with Yoshi and Tamara towards the railway station and we found the others. The children and Giles stocked up on drinks and snacks for the journey, and then we followed him, Pied Piper fashion, to a large waiting room after several diversions up and down escalators. We didn't need to remain sitting there long, however, as passengers soon started boarding the train.

The next morning we arrived in a busy, slightly foggy, but not-as-much-of-either-as-I-had-been-expecting, Beijing. Two weeks previously, my husband had heard on the Finnish news that the pollution level for this capital city was at its highest. It seemed to have subsided somewhat. It was also remarkably warm for the time of year according to the averages that I had checked on the Internet only recently. A taxi-ride, the driver in a cage, followed by a walk, brought us to the back streets amidst tiny shops and the local police station. Checking in seemed to take forever and everyone was feeling the lack of sleep and the tensions that new situations, including language barriers, invariably bring. We carried our luggage through a courtyard, passing what looked like a bronze Victorian statue, which, on later examination, turned out to be painted plastic. How much of this vast country was similarly counterfeit? The suite of rooms we had been given was on the third floor. Up we trudged with our luggage, some of us, namely me, panting for breath at the top, only to find that it wasn't as big as Giles had been expecting. They had stayed here the previous summer with Yoshi's family and had been planning the same set-up for us. As we looked around, Giles dashed back down to remedy the situation. It wasn't a complete waste of time and energy, as Tamara got a good shot of the courtyard from the window. Weeks later, when I was sorting the photos, I had wondered how we got such a scene, as from then on we were on ground level – with *no* views from the windows.

When we got to our new room, we were greeted by a combined living and dining area, a kitchenette, a bathroom, two

bedrooms, and three television sets – ample space and amenities for the six of us, and again I was grateful that hotels seem
to think that single people are square-shaped. Breakfast was
included in the price, which was generous, as the rooms were
fairly cheap. Coffee was available, which was all that concerned
me at that point in my life. The children took no time to find
the public computer in the communal area as I arranged our
bags and found extra quilts for the beds. Now we were ready to
venture out.

Christmas decorations adorned the sides of buildings, and
those at ground level promised a light show after dusk. I
remembered the email that my Chinese pen pal had sent me,
in which he had said that people in China were now more
aware of Western festivals. 'When you go out, you can see some
Christmas decorations in shopping areas. But to compare with
Hong Kong, Christmas is still not a big festival here. When we
were there last week, we could see more of the Western influence.' We wandered the main thoroughfare, each tall building
being of a different design. Quite easy to get your bearings if
you like playing *Spot the Shape*.

The shopping mall we entered could have been anywhere in
the world, apart from the prices, of course, and the ornate characters that filled the adverts and shop signs. I bought a birthday
card for my granddaughter who would be four years old soon
after Christmas. Later, we all signed it, but it didn't reach the
post until the day before her special one.

In the evening, we went back to the same area and made our
way to a restaurant on the top floor, where the chef cooked your
food before your eyes, great dollops of butter and litres of oil
being used to prepare the food you had chosen. It was delicious,
but as I usually avoid too much fat in my diet, quite disheart-
ening, in more ways than one.

Earlier in the day, Giles had asked us which we would prefer
to do on Christmas Eve, visit the Forbidden City or one section

of the Great Wall. He knew that in Finland, Eves are celebrated more than Days and wanted it to be memorable. There was no choice in our minds, hence the next day, 23 December, found us in front of Mao's huge portrait that stares out over Tiananmen Square. The area was crowded with Chinese, most seeming to want their photo taken under the famous face.

Prior to that, we three girls had done some shopping on our own. Yoshi managed well with her Chinese to get us where we wanted, and one taxi driver had been highly amused by her pronunciation and made up for some of the sourpusses we had encountered previously. One family stopped us on the pavement, wanting a photo of Tamara with their younger-than-her son, who shyly stood in front of his father for the occasion. This would happen several times, and I sometimes wonder where her pictures have been displayed and whether in the future she might, by pure coincidence, see them somewhere.

It was a chilly day as we entered the gates of the City, trying to imagine life as it used to be, beautifully portrayed in the movie, *The Last Emperor*. A ramp through an ornate archway led to a courtyard surrounded by rooms and closets, which led to another ramp through an archway … I lost count of how many times we traversed that route. Some of the buildings had already been renovated, their paintwork shining in the weak winter sun. Others were still surrounded by scaffolding, tiny dots of men without helmets or safety gear hanging on as they dismantled it, ready to start on yet another. The whole of Beijing was in preparation for the event for which there was a countdown to the nearest second on the Square. Would they be ready? I had my doubts about the taxi drivers.

Venturing into one of the many rooms that were open along the sides of the courtyards, I saw artefacts, scrolls, and other objects from Imperial Days. I could have spent more time in these spaces, but the children found it too static, so I didn't try again on my own. We did, however, all venture into an exhibit about the concubines, although I'm not sure how Giles explained to the boys what their role was in the royal household. Near the end of our time in China, I bought – may the authorities forgive me – a copy of *The Queen* on DVD. It hadn't even reached Finnish cinemas at the time I watched it in my living room, and I still haven't phoned the number I should have, if I had followed the instructions that scrolled across the screen every five minutes. I'm not quite sure how *they* managed it, but the sub-titles in English must have been a translation from another language's translation. Princess Diana was referred to as *Anna* throughout, and her title changed to *The Imperial Concubine.* When the Prime Minister's wife was addressed by the Queen's butler with, 'Would you please sit there, Mrs Blair,' the caption read, 'you please sit down Blair's madam.' Female roles seem to have been hard to pin down.

I would have needed many hours on my own to see the site of the Forbidden City properly. As it was, I had to think about where the others were and whether I was holding up the expedition. The structural designs were artistic and ornate; the curved corners of the roofs reached up to the sky with intricate carved animals adorning the passageway of roof tip to toe. Some of the pavement we walked on was mosaic, subtle colours under our feet. The trees were brown and dull, but they must turn the place into a leafy landscape in the summer.

We couldn't help but be amused by some of the signs:

Peculiar Cultural Artwork – how strange *was* it, we wondered?

Touring Souvenirs – did they pull a caravan behind them?

Watching Telephone – who was it spying on?

With working air conditioner – why was the adjective necessary?

Needing some nourishment, we sauntered into a café catering mainly to foreigners, it seemed. The young staff were dressed in Santa hats and waistcoats and looked out of place in this ancient monument to times gone by when it had been a world within a city.

Leaving the grounds at the opposite end of the site to where we had entered, we were warned by a notice that our visit was over, and if we wanted to go back through, we would have to buy some more tickets. We crossed the moat that surrounds the City and walked along the wide pavements lined with trees in hibernation mode. Getting two taxis proved quite a problem, but gave us some time to watch Beijing go by – modern buses and cars interspersed with ancient-looking bicycles carrying more than humans on their frames. How they managed to balance, pedal, and steer at the same time was a mystery to me. After much hailing, we landed in the backwaters amidst small clothes shops and cafés. One proclaimed its name in white on black, Shut Up Just Drink – not exactly welcoming. The lake nearby was frozen, and as the sun disappeared, many fairy lights twinkled on its surface. We entered a small, needing-a-coat-of-paint establishment – no particular reason why this one and not that – and ordered hot drinks to warm our chilled bones. There were four tables surrounded by settees, and the deep pink walls were covered in paintings, including one of an English cottage and stream looking lost. Maybe it was meant to make some of us feel at home.

Wandering the narrow streets later, we met a model Santa playing a saxophone by a decorated tree, his reindeer patiently waiting for his command to be off. Yoshi and Tamara couldn't resist sitting on the animals, their straw backs giving way under the human weight. Each back street was different, and little shops offered everything from electrical goods to earrings. A life-size, blown-up figure of one of the Olympic mascots caught our eye, and we realised that it was the entrance to a large department store. It was busy, but I doubted if people were buying Christmas presents. Both Tamara and I needed some relief, so we searched for a sign, and having spied it, we followed. We were directed down escalators, none having the notice that we had seen in Shanghai, saying, *Do not cling the partition board by your foot*. We seemed to be zigzagging across the floors attracting attention as foreign faces still do. Trying to ignore the stares and avoid the many stands of goods, we located the loo. The toilet was not on general view, but as we turned the corner, facing us in full view, was a female worker squatting over the hole. We looked at each other and turned tail. 'Not that desperate,' our eyes agreed.

We chose to have a Thai meal that evening, which was very tasty; the small space in which we sat was warmed by some black substance burning in a cauldron in the middle. We would see much more ornate versions, but this one was plain and utilitarian. Here the toilet was also Chinese but hidden behind a door – full-sized and hinged – that proclaimed that it housed a *Toilit*. Our self-imposed torture came to an end.

◦◦◦

'It can't be that one, it's too big!' Nonetheless, it was – a twenty-seater for six of us, plus driver and his companion, for the day's outing, as ordered by our hotel. Christmas Eve had dawned several hours before, and the Great Wall at Simitai awaited us.

The countryside flashed past as we drove out of the city, brown and dusty, unkempt and lost. Such a shame that winter would be the only time we could visit the Wall, but lack of heat and biting midges may have compensated for the lack of greenery. After a few hours, the turrets and the Wall itself came into view and it looked to be at a much higher altitude than I had imagined it would be. 'How did they manage to get their building materials up there?' I pondered.

The sun shone, a coldish breeze blew, and I knew that this would be once in a lifetime for me. Maybe the youngsters would make it again, but there were far too many places I had yet to see, and too few years in which to travel, for me to return.

Hardly any tourists were around, which was the main reason that Giles had chosen this stretch of the Wall, and one stall-holder selling fruit and snacks was shouting to us before our feet had even touched the ground. I hoped that they made enough in summer to compensate for the lack of winter customers. We found a Chinese-style, but clean, toilet block, and then the ticket office. As at the Forbidden City, we paid our four euros for adults and two for children and set off up the paved path to the base of the Wall. Ahead of us, we saw a group of Chinese, bags over shoulders, looking not at the Wall, but at us. As we passed them, their bodies swivelled to face the same direction as our noses, and their feet fell into step with ours. They tried to talk to us, and Giles attempted a few words in return. I thought they would soon become disheartened by our lack of interest, but nothing deterred them.

The Wall itself was hard going for me. Steps were unevenly sized and could slope in every direction possible. My eyes became glued to the ground, unless I stopped to survey the stunning scenery, which happened more often for me than the others. Many have tried to describe the majesty and awesomeness of the Wall, but nothing compares to the real thing. It is only when you stop at one of the watchtowers and look back over the last half-hour of your life that you recognise how twisted the barrier is, almost curling back on itself and then continuing, reminding you of a snake slithering through the undergrowth.

Two of the women who had become our uninvited compan-ions took it upon their shoulders to help me on my journey, and many times I was glad of their support at my elbows as I became dizzy from the height, the climb, and the splendour. If they hadn't tagged along, I do hope that someone from my party would have helped me in the same way. Not wanting to spoil the fun, I decided to make a stop at one of the towers and let the others continue to the top. As their voices grew fainter and their bodies disappeared from view, there was stillness and quiet, and I could almost hear my heart beating – ten to the dozen by this time. My two helpers had elected to stay and keep me company, and it wasn't long before their hands were in their bags and withdrawing books and photo scrolls. I didn't want to get into any haggling on my own, so I pointed to my bag, a large black shoulder variety slung diagonally across my body, full of emergency kit supplies and other necessities for life in an unknown world, and shook my head. Two palms and one set of eyebrows upturned finished the conversation. At the time, I didn't think that this would give them, two guardian angels in a vast wilderness, an incentive to stay with me. The ground I was standing on pitched away on both sides, only low walls providing barriers and a perch for my backside when I needed to take the weight off my feet. The sun was shining, but after the sweaty climb, I soon felt chilly. The mountains in the distance were breathtaking, shrouded in mist, one caressing the next like a row of misshapen books. Colours changed as the sun hit different areas, and the sky altered course. I had no camera to capture the various scenarios and combinations, only my memory to store them in, to reopen at times of need. For several years, I have tried, not always successfully, to live in the moment – not plagued by the past or fretting about the future – and these were surroundings that lent themselves to such an attempt. I felt small amidst the vastness, and yet very special, as though I had been handed a gift of precious jewels. No, that's too poetic, and diamonds have never interested me. They need to be locked up out of sight and can still be stolen. My treasure is a space in time, which of necessity is also hidden, but can never be taken because it resides in my heart.

Few people came up or down during the hour of my vigil, and they only required a nod or smile of recognition from me, each reciprocated gesture saying – what an awesome place. The

two Chinese women stood together at a distance, waiting for
such time as I was ready to repay them for their unsolicited kindness. However grand the experience, my heart skipped a beat
when I saw my family coming over the brow of the hill, wending
their way down to join me. The dots in the distance became
clearer and larger until we were all together again. As they had
been descending to meet me, my whole life had seemed to race
before my eyes. There had been too many partings and reunions, which could, and should, have been avoided and would
have been if only things had been different. My focusing on the
moment is still in the practising stage. But what is the saying,
'practice makes perfect'?

During their time together at the furthest part of the Wall
that was accessible, my dear, darling family had decided how
they intended to end this part of the journey, and it had not
been part of my plans, I can assure you. First of all, I thought
they were joking. I was forever falling for Giles's teasing, and
it seemed to have rubbed off on the serious Finns amongst us.
Conversely, this time, it was no jest. We continued the descent,
but then, instead of following the path we had come up on,
they took a side turning. Our Chinese followers knew that this
was the parting of the ways and hastily removed their goods,
including books, T-shirts, scroll-like panoramic views, and postcards. We bought some items after the obligatory haggling, and
I made a final gesture by thrusting some notes into the hands of
one of my helpers. She seemed surprised, but whether because
it was a lot or too little, I shall never know.

The short path brought us to a metal stage suspended over
the side of the mountain, manned by an almost round personage
in a huge army coat. Below us, a river wound its way between
the hills without a care in the world. Two sets of metal cables
stretched into the winter air and disappeared into the future.

Giles and Yoshi each stepped into a harness and were hooked together onto one of the pairs of wires. By this time, they were on the edge of the platform, and not the one nearest safety. The disguised attendant pushed them into squatting position and told them, I imagine, to push off – which they did, sliding away from us, down and down, further and further away. I couldn't believe my eyes, or that I was expected to follow them in this adventure. Too soon for me, another set of harnesses arrived, and Timo and Tamara were buckling up. As they grew smaller and smaller in the distance, Tamara's red coat a burst of colour in the dreary winter landscape, I saw our transport arriving. Thomas, armed with our camcorder, and I buckled up and were soon hurtling through space, twisting and turning as we had no choice but to allow the metal ropes to do their job. It had been almost impossible to bend my knees at the boundary of that launching pad, even harder to push off with my feet. Was it my imagination that we had been given a friendly shove? I didn't know where to look – up, down, across, or at Thomas's coat. The short journey was invigorating, and I felt glad that the choice had been taken away from me. The thought of trudging the downhill path on my own had seemed almost as daunting as this situation. The landing stage came in sight, and we were supposed to bend our knees to arrive correctly. Mine would not obey the commands my brain was trying to convey, and Thomas and I seemed caught up in an endless dance. Boots finally struck metal, and we were unhitched, by whom I have no recollection. My whole body felt like jelly, and I'm sure I was exhibiting my nervous laughter that appears at non-appropriate times.

After a short walk, we found a frozen expanse of water, and Giles set up his tiny tripod and camera on it, checking for the background and angle. We crouched down in a row, the Wall away in the distance behind us and thanks to time-delays, we now have a wonderful shot of our special Christmas Eve outing. I also managed to get quite a few of the countryside as we made the return journey to Beijing. They came out well, considering that we were moving as I took them, although they would have been more pleasing to the eye if the scenery had been greener. Small clusters of houses gave way to nothing but barrenness, and then a large modern building would come into view. Not much further along would be a row of tumbledown workshops, rubbish spilling out of bins, piles of bricks and debris adorning the street. We passed bicycles, some with loads reaching the sky, others with human burdens riding side-saddle on the back. Timber lorries flew past, the logs cut into uniform lengths and carried sideways across the truck, unlike in Finland where the trees of various sizes are transported lengthways. As we neared the city proper, the number of vehicles increased, and we were soon caught in a mild traffic jam. I didn't recognise the surroundings when we stopped without warning, and the driver turned round expecting us to alight. Giles tried to remonstrate and started pointing to the other side of the large highway, I presumed to where we had been picked up that morning. The driver, a young man in his twenties, started shouting, and the children and I didn't know if we should move or not. Who was the boss here? When the driver joined us in the back and was almost eyeball to eyeball with Giles, we all decided that this was the best place to get out. We had a walk back to the hotel – and discovered our surprises.

On our beds were four red and white furry hats with our names on sticky labels. Each one contained some small presents, including a tiny wooden chest of drawers, the top inlaid with mother-of-pearl, which I now use for jewellery, Christmas tissues, sweets, and for the children some rubbery, squidgy shapes with plastic eyes, which could be pushed into grotesque, or cute, shapes. Later, we discovered that these were filled with a white substance like talcum powder, as one of Tamara's new plastic friends objected to the continual squeezing and moulding and burst all over the bed and floor.

I felt sad because I had left our presents in Shanghai and hadn't bought any more in Beijing for Giles and Yoshi, worrying that there wouldn't be room in their luggage. After all, we still had many plans.

Having rested, washed, and changed, we set off, Christmas hats on heads, through the busy streets of Beijing to find a place for our Christmas meal. We found a new restaurant called Sixth Sense, serving only Japanese food. The prices were higher than other places, but hey, it was Christmas. The food was served on varying-shaped plates, artistically arranged, and it was delicious. A cold breeze wafted over our legs every time the door opened, but I suppose you can't get everything right all of the time.

Next morning most of us slept late while I quietly made an instant cup of coffee that I drank with some Chinese-style crackers. Our main shopping day lay ahead, and by the end of it, I would be wishing that I had brought my autumn shoes with me instead of leaving them in Shanghai. All I had were my winter boots, retractable spikes on the bottoms, one size too big to allow for chunky woollen socks over thick tights, requisite wear for an average Finnish winter. So far into our trip, the weather had been much milder than I had anticipated, and the temperature in the indoor market would be even higher. I decided to wear only socks, which proved to be shorter than the tops of my boots. On our return that evening, I primarily blamed the blameless elastic in the tops of the socks, but on further scrutiny, it dawned on me that the red, raw rings had been caused by my feet floating around all day within receptacles that should have been airtight. The elasticised bandage I was carrying with me in case a vein burst in a leg was cut in two and was in constant use for the rest of our trip. The tube of soothing cream didn't last that long.

We all ate a late breakfast in a clean, modern shop selling all kinds of pastries and cakes. Grab your tray and a pair of tongs, and away you go; the cashier dispenses your choice of drink and for less than the price of a cookie at home, you are replete. Stomachs full, we stood at a busy junction and hailed two taxis. On getting out, my eye was caught by a large poster on the side of the road proclaiming that 'Provence is over the shore, but your buffalo is not.' I'm still working on that one.

The indoor market was immense, one floor on top of the next, one cubicle after another, selling just about everything you might need. Prices started off low by Western, or crazily high by Chinese standards, but bargaining was expected and often took far longer than necessary. I decided to buy a suitcase. How long do you think that took, including walking away, having another stallholder rush at me with a similar case to the one I had been haggling over, only to have the original girl shout across the crowds that my last offer was acceptable? At least thirty minutes I guess, although I didn't set a timer. The children got some good offers on clothes that are still in shape, of the original colour with logos intact, three months on. That can't be said for everything, however. Tamara's T-shirt with *Hard Rock Café, Shanghai* emblazoned on the front lost most of its wording after the first wash, and it looked more like she was swearing, so we had to remove some more to make it acceptable. Please don't spend too long trying to imagine what peeled off and what didn't. In addition, her *I climbed the Great Wall of China* T-shirt looks as though she is trying to hide the fact. You would embarrass yourself, and her, if you got as close as you would need to, to read the faint, whitish ghosts that are all that remain of the letters. Belts, bracelets, fans, slippers, sports trousers, sweat shirts, T-shirts, trainers, underwear, and a small metal tool for their father in Finland, not forgetting my luggage, all made its way from there back to our hotel. And no doubt, I've forgotten something ... oh yes, a blue, short-sleeved Chinese-style tunic for Tamara, off the peg, as it were.

I was carrying nearly fifty postcards, all written on, plus an enveloped birthday card for our granddaughter and niece in my bag in the hopes of finding a post office. When we finally emerged into – what was it, not daylight and certainly not fresh air? – the open, we stumbled along the pavement with our acquired supplies looking for a suitable place to buy stamps and post letters. It had just closed.

It was late when we got back to the hotel, but there was still one more surprise provided by Giles and Yoshi for this extraordinary and unforgettable Christmas – a round, white loaf of bread with nine lettered candles which were soon alight, wishing us all, with correct spelling, although abbreviated, a 'Merry Xmas'.

Chapter 5

Lijiang

Streams and Souvenirs

We crossed the tiny bridge over a stream, the glow from red lanterns reflected on its surface. After piling our cases and backpacks in a corner, we studied the menu that a young woman dressed in the national costume of the local minority people, the Naxis, brought to us.

The People's Republic of China officially recognizes fifty-six ethnic groups, one of which is the Naxi, also spelled Nahki, Naqxi or Nasi, depending on which book or web page you look at. They are thought to have come from Tibet originally and certainly share some of their features. They seem proud of their Dongba script, a form of pictograph writing using over 1,400 symbols. I bought a three-way dictionary of Dongba, Chinese, and English printed on special paper made by them, the craft of which is dying by the second, and we were all fascinated by the stylised caricatures. The one for diarrhoea caught the children's eye and caused a few guffaws. Today, fewer than a hundred Dongba priests can read and write this ancient language because of its suppression during the Cultural Revolution, but there are efforts to have its learning returned to the school curriculum.

Many of the older women still wear their traditional clothes, only face and hands exposed to the air. Blue, white, and maroon seemed to be the dominant colours, as they danced their slow dance in two circles in one of Lijiang's squares on our last day there. The sun was shining, and we were waiting to collect our belongings and leave for Shanghai, the end of our trip in sight, but there are more stories to tell before we arrived back there.

That initial night was our first sight of these people as the young woman handed us a menu. Giles and Yoshi had disappeared to find us somewhere to stay for the night. I felt relieved that we were in mobile phone contact and couldn't imagine the life my father, and many others like him, endured, with only mule-mail. News must have been so stale by the time it reached its destination, unlike in our modern world where every second can be accounted for.

When the room-hunters returned, we were eating noodles – green, glutinous ones – not what I thought would arrive when I placed the order oh so confidently. The hot chocolate was creamy and sour tasting, and I wondered if this was because it had been made with yak's milk. It was late and way past our normal eating hours, but daily routines had already flown out of the window, which was easy in this environment as the night breezes blew through the empty frames beside the table.

Trundling and carrying our luggage, we followed Giles through the cobbled streets until we arrived at a covered doorway leading into a courtyard, so characteristic of this country. There were three double rooms available, each with its own tiny shower room and electric blankets on the beds. My half didn't work, but an extra layer of clothes did the job. The door to our room consisted of six concertina-panels, the top halves carved with dragons, and Tamara discovered how to lock it from the inside; one simply pushed the wooden wedge under it. The padlock for the outside lay on the cupboard waiting for our departure.

As I lay in another strange bed, surrounded by unfamiliar noises, my thoughts wandered back through the day. It had started with a late breakfast in the clean, fresh bakery we had eaten at two days earlier – or was it only yesterday? – which had been followed by a taxi ride to Beijing's domestic airport, where I had relieved the weight of my shoulder bag by posting the numerous postcards, and then we had checked in and waited for the flight which would take us to the south-west of the country. At Kunming airport, in Yunnan Province, several hours later, we had been ordered off the plane, and during this cleaning break, I had lost the notebook and pen that Thomas had neatly stowed in the net of the seat in front. Re-embarkation had been followed by a short hop to Lijiang airport, where we had waited in the dark in a small public bus for a ride into the town itself. We had been deposited in a small courtyard which we had exited to find some taxis, out of which we had tumbled to walk with our luggage through the most magical area I had ever seen, complete with fairy lights twinkling in the trees. Following our leader, we had ordered green noodles from a young woman dressed as in a travel brochure. And now here I was, lying next to Tamara, sleepless in Lijiang.

Next morning I was surprised to find flowers blooming in pots in the central area of the hotel, unless that is too grand a word for where we had slept. In Finland, we hadn't seen any colour for several months. From their experience earlier, Giles and Yoshi knew that we could find somewhere better to stay. He paid for our night, dirt cheap, but more than they would have got if we hadn't turned up out of the blue in the early hours of the morning, and we set off with our worldly goods to hunt. What we found were two triple rooms, one on each end of a carpeted first floor corridor that was open to the elements on one side, and again I thanked hotels for their belief that all guests are as wide as they are tall. Nights were cold, and the small wall heater seemed rather inadequate for its task, but as I tried to keep warm next to Tamara, I decided this was preferable to intense heat and mosquitoes.

The following morning, we went to a cute little café for a late breakfast and then spent the day wandering the narrow cobbled streets, watching every footstep as the polished stones dipped in all directions, crossing the tiny streams sometimes teaming with goldfish, and haggling for handiwork both for ourselves and as presents. The list of names of people who I wanted to buy gifts for, which I had carefully made at home, had now disappeared in Kunming's disposal system, unless it was, at this moment, being translated by our very thorough cleaner. I had also copied into that notebook some nonsensical English from signs in Shanghai, Beijing, and the trains in between and hoped that those were not being used for English practice.

The old town of Lijiang, since 1997 a UNESCO World Heritage site, is beautiful, but thanks to *Lonely Planet,* it is not quite alone anymore. Then again, it wasn't only foreign tourists thronging the place. There were many Chinese groups, their guides waving little flags above their heads as they proceeded through this well-kept, until now, secret. Most wanted their photo taken by the two water wheels that proclaim the border of the ancient part of town. Nearby was a wooden board that exhorted the residents, and visitors, one presumed, in Chinese, English, and Dongba, to *Be patriotic and Law-abiding.* There were also instructions to *Unite and friendly, Hard-working and thrifth and live on one's own,* and *Have good sence and keep one's word.* Mountains bound the whole area, and you couldn't go far without seeing one sandwiched between the tilting roofs of neighbouring buildings.

One evening we decided to go to a folksy café for dinner. It was mainly a drinking place, but food was also served. On a raised platform in the bay window, musicians came and went, singing and playing a variety of styles and languages. I was surprised when, at one point, I realised I was listening to Korean and was only able to understand one word, the one for love.

My teenage years had been busy with school, part-time work,

and church activities, and even when I embarked on my college career, Folk Club met on the same evening as the Christian Union, which I had to attend. At that juncture in my life, no force on earth could have kept me away. As I sat there, the oldest face in the place, I was in reality much younger and basking in the wonder and thrill of live music. I couldn't help singing along with the ones I knew, but I tried to keep it as quiet as possible. My youngest children would have been highly embarrassed – maybe they were anyway – and maybe they also pretend to their friends that I am their grandparent, as I did with my father.

He had been fifty-six when I was born; not exactly in his prime. After his return from China, he had travelled around Britain as an itinerant preacher, going wherever and whenever he was asked. Consequently, he had been away from home a lot. Sometimes, though, on the rare occasions when he had been able to, he had come to meet me after school.

A friend shouts to me from the doorway to the playground. 'Your grandfather's here for you, Ruth.'

I needed to make this trip to Lanping, the town he had devoted his best years to, to tell him how sorry I was that I hadn't claimed him as my father – that I had kept my mouth shut and let them go on believing that the greying man was one generation behind his real role in my life. When he had died shortly after, I had felt ashamed, but it was too late to make amends. None of us know when the last sight, touch, and word will be.

How to get to Lanping? The crunch of this trip was approaching, and the butterflies felt eager for release. We decided that the best way would be to hire a vehicle and driver, and if he couldn't speak English, another person to act as interpreter. Giles entered several travel establishments, not typical Western offices, but small spaces with covered walls offering, in unique

English, trips to the local sights. Lanping was not one of them, and some workers hadn't even heard of the place, so it obviously wasn't a tourist destination.

After various encounters, one young lady was willing to phone her head office – but please remove the image of a sparkling skyscraper from your mind – although, as she connected, we had no idea what she was doing. She handed the phone to Giles who was able to speak in English to the person at the other end, and we were soon headed through the narrow lanes to what we hoped would be a larger place that could produce the goods. It was bigger, but still basic, and this young woman could talk the lingo. She was surprised at our request but could see that we were serious, so she retrieved her pile of possible drivers from the drawer and started her phone calls. I'm not sure how many she tried before she had success, but by the time we left, we had secured the services of a bus and driver for two days, plus a young woman whom they found. We asked the one in the office to join us, but she would be busy. As it turned out, that would be a disappointment.

Chapter 6

Lanping

Wishes and Waiting

I show her the aging photo of a middle-aged man in a dishevelled suit standing outside a doorway, and as I point to him, with a quiver of emotion in my voice, I say the only word that she might understand.

'Harry?'

She smiles.

Her finger, wrinkled and worn with age, points up the lane.

It wasn't that easy, but not exactly difficult either, looking back – much like life itself. At the start of this trip, all I had were some old photos from the 1930s and 40s and a few more of when my oldest brother Alfred, who had been born in Lanping in 1930, had made a visit there with his son, Martin, in 1997. I had phoned my nephew in Australia before our departure and it had all sounded easy. The old house was near the hospital, and people only had to hear the word Harry – with the added bonus of the speaker having a Western face I suppose – and everyone knew who was being referred to. How we had wished.

We had set off at eight from the travel agency in a white minibus, the driver in his thirties, looking extremely confident with himself. He had a friend in Lanping and knew where we were going, which was comforting to know. We had gleaned this information from the young woman who was accompanying us. They were both intrigued about our trip, and she asked questions, and he asked some more, which she translated. Her English was basic, but we would have to trust that what she transferred, both ways, was somewhere near the truth.

About half an hour out of Lijiang, the minibus came to a halt, and an ornate gateway was pointed out to us. It was clear that we were expected to get out, which we dutifully did. Through the arched entrance, we could see on the mountainside facing us, a kind of temple shining in the early morning sun. A tourist attraction for the Chinese themselves apparently, as a coach was parked nearby, but it seemed the passengers had other interests as they headed for a group of metal cabins on the other side of the road, which was quite civilised for this country.

The mandatory photos taken, we continued on our way, a hundred kilometres if the by-now-exhausted crow flew there, but more than double that as we wound round the mountains, breath-taking views awaiting us beyond each bend, villages nestled in the valleys, red soil clinging to the mountainsides. I tried not to look down or at the road as we overtook slow-moving trucks at blind spots.

We passed through small hamlets, tumbledown houses lining the street, metal shutters covering entrances to courtyards, children wandering around, men sitting in groups, and women with piles on their backs. One time it was a statue-making community; white rock and stones lined the road and piled behind workers who looked as though they had been dusted with icing sugar. Then there would be only fields and rice terraces, barren at this time of year, waiting for spring to burst into life.

I felt as though I was on another personal journey from winter to spring. The previous one had taken far too long to complete as I had clung to the role of victim for survival, not understanding at the time that no one can make a person feel what she doesn't want to. As individuals, all people are in charge of their own thoughts, and they cannot blame anyone else for how they feel about their situation or themselves. However, I am jumping ahead of myself – those thoughts have only clarified while I have been writing about this trip. At the time, I was still dealing with my childhood losses and lack of memories. I needed to touch base with my father and find the place where he had invested so much of himself.

After several hours of hair-raising bends, inferior suspension, and stunning views of the blue, cloudy sky through steamed up, perspiring windows, we were told that we were entering Lanping. I think I had been expecting a small town, but this place spread out like an oak tree. Buildings flashed by on each side of us, blue roadside walls painted with large white Chinese characters – is it advertising or propaganda? is there a difference? – and we strained our necks to get a glimpse of this place that had filled my imagination for too many years.

The centre of town was huge and sprawling; modern shops, by Chinese standards, surrounded us, and cars and trucks hooted as they tried to avoid the mules, which were also traversing these roads, laden baskets hanging at their sides. The sun shone on the mix of old and new, the 30 km/h speed signs and the zebra crossings. I can remember wondering what animal they called them after here.

As Martin had said to look for the hospital, that was what the driver asked for and where we arrived, bang in the middle of civilization, no vegetation in sight, or at least nothing that could spring to life in a few months time. This was nothing like the photos from nine years ago, which showed trees and bushes in abundance, and my heart dropped. This was not going to be as easy as I had imagined.

What I had failed to register was that when Martin had been here with his father, he had been with my brother, who spoke and understood Chinese. It might have seemed like a stroll in the park for them to find the old Fisher residence, but without a doubt, Alfred had been able to talk the walk into his past. We didn't have that luxury. Anyway, was I barging into my other older siblings' lives like the oft-maligned bull in a china shop? I am a Taurus after all. I had been telling my children that I was making this trip, one that developed into a pilgrimage the closer I got to our goal, not just for myself and them, but also for my brothers and sister who had been born here, and Giles had asked me, I think tongue in cheek, 'Are you sure they want you to?' It was a good question; I hadn't asked them, and they hadn't made the request of me. Was I assuming too much to think that they would even care I was doing this? Maybe it was all one big ego trip.

Pushing my self doubts back where they belonged, we continued the search. I suggested to the driver, through the girl, that we all stop for lunch somewhere and continue our inquiries afterwards. We parked near a 'restaurant' open to the street, low tables and benches mostly occupied, and those that were not were full of dirty dishes and wasted food. I must admit that I hoped the leftovers wouldn't be recycled to us. I'm not that into 'waste not, want not'. We sat down, and Giles, Yoshi, and the girl ordered some food, while the driver disappeared to another table with my photos. They were mainly young people around, and I felt in my heart that it would be an older person who would be able to direct us to my father's former abode, someone who would have been a child at that time and had heard stories about the 'white westerners' or 'foreign devils', depending on their family's viewpoint.

Lunch was not the best we had had – the dishes too liquid to eat comfortably with chopsticks – but we all persevered. The toilet, up a flight of outside steps, was also overflowing, but just as hunger had won the battle downstairs, our stomachs and waste tracts did the same into the hole in the concrete.

Our driver seemed more confident about where we should go, so off we went, some squiggles on a piece of paper our passport to the promised land. There were some more stops and puzzled expressions as various vendors were asked the way. Out of the centre, we passed walls, trees, and paths, all an assortment of shades of brown. Then out of nowhere, there would be tall, cream buildings nodding to the fact that we were in the twenty-first century. Lines of small vans adorned the kerbs as the sky darkened, and ominous clouds floated through the sky. Shacks flashed passed the windows, untidy and neat standing side by side, intermittently interrupted by moving lorries and buses, the view constantly changing and matching the emotions in my heart.

As we stopped in the more ancient part of town, I saw from the minibus two older women up a short flight of steps, seemingly passing the time of day, maybe neighbours discussing their grandchildren's progress at school or the latest price of rice. Somehow, I knew that they would know.

⋅☙⋅

Thinking about that time now, I feel as though I'm re-living those emotions of longing for, and needing to find, my father. I jump out of the vehicle and run up the steps, a photo of my father taken just before his departure from this place, maybe a stone's throw from where my feet now touch the earth, clutched in my hands. My heart is thumping, and I feel as though my whole life depends on finding the house that my father had called home long before the collection of bricks and mortar that he and I had given that name to existed.

There is only one word that these women might have in common with me, not one that I used as a child, but one that I have only recently started using because too many people cannot call him Dad as I do. My hands trembling, I show her the sixty-two-year-old photo of a middle-aged white man, hands behind his back, trying to resign himself to the fact that he has to leave his beloved adopted country because the Japanese are now too close for comfort. What thoughts are ploughing through his mind as he stands outside the home he has made for his family? Is he thinking about his wife and baby daughter buried somewhere in the area, his local congregation of Chinese believers, the many American servicemen he has brought back to health and safety during the previous years? Is he concerned about his journey back to England with five children and what awaits them there?

'Harry?'

My pronunciation might not be Chinese, but my skin is the correct colour, and we have finally arrived in the right area of town – what might have been the original. Her smile tells me all I need to know, and mine tries to thank her for being one of the last pieces of this part of the puzzle to be fitted into place.

I don't know when the others join us, only that we are all walking slightly uphill past red brick walls with drainage channels beneath them and rickety corrugated roofs above, following someone who senses what we want to find. Another corner, another gate opens into a courtyard, where are we going? We emerge from a narrow alley and see blocks of white flats on our right, open to the sky. Turning left, we walk uphill along a dusty path towards a gate with a sloping roof. There's a pair of large wooden doors in front of us, each one adorned with the same Chinese character, walls on each side – impossible to know what's inside this fortress. Sensing that we are near the end of our search, Yoshi puts her arm around me, and we watch together as our driver gingerly opens the gate, peers inside, and shouts. A dog barks in reply from a courtyard showing bright yellow doors higher than eye-level. We are a party of eight with four nationalities represented – English, Finnish, Sri Lankan and Chinese, and seem to take over the space that only seconds before had been slumbering in the winter sunshine. No one knows we are coming. This is a surprise visit from the past, opening what kind of memories for the inhabitants of this pin-prick area of planet earth?

The next few hours go by in a haze. An elderly gentleman, whom I recognise from Martin's photos taken nine years previously, emerges from a doorway on a raised area opposite the main gate. We learn his name – I shall call him Mr Li, and he talks about his childhood and our photos and his pictures, both those adorning the walls of his room and some in a small album.

'It looks as though he's looked through these many times,' I venture saying to anyone who might be listening, but I doubt that such off-the-cuff remarks are even registered, let alone translated.

The aged and newer photos that I had compiled in plastic wallets sit side by side, spread out on a long wooden bench, as he explains who the people in his treasure are. He uses a lot more words than we receive. Our driver speaks no English, and the girl has a finite vocabulary, and anyway, he is speaking ten to the dozen as his teenage grandson hovers, wondering what has exploded into his quiet afternoon. Tamara discovers a small dog that is overjoyed to have some personal attention. The larger one, which barked a welcome or warning on our arrival, is held prisoner within a confined space – a large wooden crate in sight of the entrance.

Opposite Mr Li's single room, which contains a bed, chair, cupboard, and tiny television, is a rundown two-storey house looking remarkably out of place in this old part of rural China. A door is in the centre, with windows on each side and above, their frames wooden and the spaces where the glass should have been, latticed. Very western. Extremely English. I know that this must be the building that my father helped to build for his family – the raw materials that had encased his heart. Would I find him here amongst the rubble and disuse?

I walk down the steps that lead to the front door, past a

barren tree with a white cap hanging on a branch, looking as though it's waiting for someone to claim it. An old, brown-stained bathtub is propped to the left of the entrance; a pile of rocks sits on the right, and my heart is pumping blood that has ached since childhood for the father who died when I was nine. My eyes take a little time to adjust to the darkness inside the house, but I can see light coming through the roof and the ceiling. As I move around, I see small signs of the past. How far back, I don't know, but can that dirty shuttlecock be sixty years old? Did one of my brothers or sisters play with it, or have other children lived and played within these walls since their departure, prompted by the proximity of Japanese forces?

The wooden ceilings are broken, gaping like open wounds, the wood pointing like spears in opposite directions. Concrete has crumbled, walls have withered, and time has taken its toll. All around us is dereliction and decay. What memories do these walls store? How many books could be written about the everyday life and dramas that were lived and breathed within this space?

On the top floor I notice an old wooden box with the word MORTON stamped on the side, and below it, almost indecipherable, another six-letter word – London. This has to be the right place. As if I need some confirmation, some external object to give credence to the flutterings and explosions in my chest.

'This is what your granddad built nearly eighty years ago.' What does that mean to the ears that hear my voice?

I have to tell someone that I am here, standing on this sacred ground, a tiny speck of earth's surface that has been held in my mind's eye since childhood. Not sure if there will be a signal, I calculate the time in England and hope that it isn't too early. My sister receives the news that I am standing in the old house one day before my siblings and their spouses will be together for their annual Christmas gathering, continued even after Mum's passing sixteen years earlier. This is the place where Faith was

born and left motherless, all on the same day, sixty-five years
earlier. What will be flooding through her soul at this moment?
Giles also speaks to her and promises that he will bring her to
see this place that has been at the heart of our family for as long
as I can remember.

᠅

Now I realise that we didn't receive much information about
what happened to the house after my family's abandoning it,
except that no one had lived in it for fifty years. Maybe I asked
more questions, but didn't get a translation of the reply, or it
wasn't one of the queries that got translated because too many
people were talking and listening and pondering and exclaiming
at once. Did the Communists commandeer the house, or did
local families make use of its emptiness? I imagine that Harry
had to leave all the family furniture behind and only took personal effects and mementoes of that stretch of time lived in an
alien environment. That would make sense of Mr Li telling us
that Harry had constructed his bed, as he beckoned me to sit
beside him. 'What memories do these walls have,' I wondered,
'and how about this furniture? Did my father make it or merely
pass on instructions in his faltering Chinese to local workers,
grateful for some extra work even though they had their fears
about fraternising with the foreigners. How long had it taken for
my gentle father and his family to be accepted by the local community?' So many questions had never been asked. When you're
nine, you have eternity – no feeling of rush, or even necessity.

Clouds hung over the mountaintops, some of them snow-
capped. What a sight to set your eyes on every morning as you
rub the sleep out of your eyes and prepare them for slumber in
the evening. How hard it must have been to leave this wonder
of nature – this little bit of heaven on earth.

Through translation, we discovered that our host wanted
to show us another place, and thinking that we would not be

returning to this present location, I took my leave of Dad by doing the only thing I could: I walked as in a funeral procession to the outside wall of the house nearest the gate, roof tiles piled against it waiting to be re-used. I laid my hand on it next to a window frame. As skin touched roughcast wall, I allowed the tears to flow. They had been many years in the making – too many. Giles saw me and came and put his arm around my shoulder. As he made that simple action, we exchanged roles, and I became the parent and he the child. Then our roles reversed again – such complex emotions flowing through our linked veins.

We followed Mr Li out of the compound, down the path we had recently trodden up, at which time we had felt uncertain of being in the right place and whether we would find the elderly gentleman who was displayed in our photos of just under a decade earlier. There was no clear translation of where we were going, but we understood that it was linked with Harry. The paths wandered and were so narrow we could almost touch the walls on each side of us with outstretched arms. After several minutes, we passed three toddler boys just finishing their affairs into the drain at the side of the path. They smiled shyly at our beaming faces, and their gazes followed us until we fell away from view around another corner. A richer doorway faced us; more elaborate and painted with red roses. 'Who lives here, and why are we here?' I wondered. We couldn't all be with the translator at the same time, so often my questions went unasked. The buildings that we passed inside the garden were more modern looking. A middle-aged lady had appeared at the barking of her dogs and led us along another path, away from her home towards a courtyard of derelict buildings, some piled high with wood ready for burning. We assumed that this area had some significance for us and soon realised that it was the place that Martin had taken many photos of; only then, there had been lots of greenery, and now there was only brown, except for one broad-leaved plant proudly strutting its stuff in a corner. Giles and I tried to find the correlation between paper and reality and soon saw some outlines that matched.

So, what was this place that we had been brought to now as Alfred and Martin had just under a decade earlier? Why had they taken many photos of this area and none of the old house we had just visited? At least none that they had felt were worth sending to England from where my sister-in-law had made and sent me copies? Was this the house that Harry had built? Had my earlier feelings of proximity to my long-departed, hard-to-remember-clearly father betrayed me and been an illusion? Had I been so desperate to find him that any building could have been fobbed off on me? Confusion filled my soul and left me breathless. What is this place?

It would be several months later, once I was back in Finland with my memories of this trip and some old photos that I had no recollection of seeing before, that the sun would shine through the cobwebs and reveal the truth. It would become so obvious once I would start thinking outside the box. Of course …

As my thoughts return to what transpired next in Lanping, my pulse is pounding. We are all, Mr Li included, sitting in our modern mule, driving back towards the town. Through the girl, we learn that we are going to see where the Gospel Hall, as I later learned that my father referred to it, was built. The streets are narrow, and the driver has to avoid pedestrians who don't seem to care that this is also a thoroughfare for vehicles. Everyone is busy. There is movement in all directions. Horns are honking, and oriental faces are staring at the foreign ones peering at this unknown world. Ahead, the road is almost canopied with colourful umbrellas shading vendors and buyers from the bright winter sunshine. It's hard to believe that this is just a few days after Christmas, as we shed a layer each.

'Surely, we are not going to venture up that street – there's hardly room for human traffic, let alone the engine variety.' Before I have time to voice my astonishment, the minibus stops outside some high metal gates. Mr Li jumps out and opens them, and we drive inside and park to the left of a huge compound. Was this it? As we descend, a huge building faces us but looks far too modern to be connected to Harry. Someone suggests 'use-of-now toilets' that are open, and some of us take advantage of the offer, trying to cover noses and mouths in the process, quite a job when you're squatting and also attempting not to touch the walls that would offer some stability to legs unaccustomed to this posture.

The rest of the party are waiting by the gates of this enclosure, and we set off after Mr Li. We turn right and walk towards the rainbow canopies, but soon the bodies of our party are disappearing around another right corner. Giles and I are bringing up the rear, and I become aware of piped Chinese singing filling the bustling market area, where an old man sits on an upturned basket in a coat and fur hat without a care in the world, surveying the sacks of rice inside a shop. In a flash, so fast that there is no time to take another breath, the music changes, and a western male voice, singing a song that I recognise but cannot immediately place, fills my ears.

Wherever you go, whatever you do,
I will be right here waiting for you.
—Richard Marx

Once before in my life, after visiting his grave in our hometown before leaving for foreign shores, my father had 'sung' to me and reassured me of his love. Here he was again, knowing that I had made this journey with trepidation and fear, but with

a deep conviction that I had to do this. If I had needed any
confirmation that I had asked the right thing of my children
to accompany me on this strange and surreal journey into the
past, here it was. I just looked at Giles, and I knew that he knew
what I was thinking and feeling. My body felt as though it was
floating, and the love that screamed through my veins almost
hurt.

On my return home, I found the Richard Marx song, 'Right
Here Waiting', that those words were from and downloaded it
– after paying – onto my computer. So curious that almost the
only part of that song that I heard in that dusty, off-the-beaten-
track Chinese town had any relevance to me and my relationship
with my father. A second earlier or later the message would have
had little impact.

Listening to the song since though has reminded me again of
the fleetingness of time. We just never know when the last sight
or sound of our loved ones will be.

⌒⌒

The walls on each side of us were tall, various shades of
white, old and flaky, and patched and worn. Mr Li was talking,
and the girl was trying to pass his words on to us. The scene
was almost unreal, as though I were watching a movie or one of
my endless dreams of trying to achieve, reach, or accomplish an
unspecified task or destination which is just beyond my grasp,
my capability.

We passed through an entrance that led to a courtyard surrounded by two-storey dwellings, the inhabitants' washing
drying on various lines that criss-crossed the open space. I felt
uncomfortable standing in this private area, nine strange bodies
amidst the everyday lives of strangers. What is this all about?
The place looked nothing like a Gospel Hall. Anyway, I had a
vague memory of a photo of the inside of this structure, and it
appeared quite western, a large, high area, but covered, full of

benches with Bible verses displayed on the walls. This space was open to the elements, no ceiling in sight. We could only guess that the church building had not survived the communist years as the house had done, and this was merely the site of the Hall – these homes built on the foundations of that labour of love.

As we re-emerged into the narrow alleyway, Mr Li started an animated story that the girl and driver listened to seriously. The translation we received in staccato fashion was as follows. (Bear in mind that the Fisher family left this town in late 1944 upon the approach of Japanese forces.)

In 1949 when Mr Li was fourteen years old, Harry had returned to Lanping, but was beaten out of the place by the locals following the orders of the communist leaders. Whether they themselves had known Harry or were newcomers was unclear. Mr Li, showing much emotion in his face, tears in his eyes, told us that he had been one of those who had been ordered to do the beating. Disobeying orders would have meant certain death.

I had never heard any stories about this return, but that wasn't surprising to me. What did *I* know about this place and my father's life? Harry had married my mother in December 1949, so it was possible that he had been in China in the earlier part of the year. My older siblings had been living in different parts of Britain and wouldn't necessarily have known what their father was doing or where he was. The first time they were all together was after my parents' marriage and the new start in what would become our hometown.

It made sense to me – Mum had been a nurse and would have been invaluable to a missionary in these circumstances. Had he been hoping to return here with his new wife and his children and start again? Did that mean that my younger brother and I would have been born here, too?

Is *this* where he wanted me to be born?

Is *that* why he's been waiting here for me?

The answers didn't matter. The truth was unimportant. I didn't care what happened all those years before – this story was for my ears. It was my reassurance that Dad loved me and was glad that I had returned to the place he had loved, the spot where he had left his heart over sixty years ago.

Before returning to the bus, Mr Li went to a market stall and purchased some strawberries and mandarins, their bright colours twinkling in the late afternoon sun. As the van passed over a small stream, we looked to our right, and Giles and I both realised at the same time why Alfred and Martin had taken photos from this vantage point. In the distance, nestled at the foot of a wooded slope, was the doorway to the old Fisher abode.

The van got us as far as it could to that entrance, and we walked the rest of the distance, the bags of fruit swinging at Mr Li's sides, inviting us to a last nostalgic sharing of food. A yellow-painted chair was produced and placed with other assorted stools and benches around a small table on the raised platform outside our host's room. I was invited to sit in the chair that had been made by or at least belonged to my father; in this instance, I played the role of the matriarch. The fruit was delicious, and someone told us that strawberries had been introduced to China by the British, one of the more pleasant imports. Below us were two winter-bare trees looking stark. We were informed that they were pear trees, brought by Harry to this place and still growing where they had been planted to provide fresh food for his family. Could they have also been a reminder of the old country and his parents' garden, or were pears his favourite fruit for an autumnal day? I will never know what importance they held for him, but speculation is fun.

Our host must have been trying to place me in a Harry context because he asked me, through the girl, if the single English lady who had been living with the family had been my mother. He must have assumed that Harry married her after their journey back to England, but I was able to assure him that Harry had found a different wife.

We left Lanping the evening of the day we had arrived, although we had been planning to stay one night. Exhaustion, both physical and emotional, had overtaken me, and I couldn't imagine driving around this place any longer, trying to find somewhere to stay – and eat. We had found what we had been searching for, in my case for a lifetime, and there would be no point in returning to the former Fisher home with the current state of translation.

As we drove out of the town, I noticed water running down a wall into the road; a missionary's tears.

Not long into our return trip, Tamara decided she needed a toilet-break. We stopped by the side of the road, and she jumped out, running as far as she could from prying eyes. A little further on our journey, we had to swerve as a herd of black goats, large and small, commandeered the road. I was relieved we hadn't been on a bend.

The driver had been almost too interested in our story, and on the return journey, I began hoping that Mr Li had known what he had been doing when he had produced a modern Chinese Bible from his room to show us, before our departure. Had he been a secret believer for all these years, and had he been persecuted for what my father had taught him, or had the book been a gift from Alfred on his visit nine years before?

Our two Chinese companions had some long discussions on that return trip. I wondered how much was real and how much guesswork. I trusted that this would be a memorable day for them and give them a different topic to talk about at mealtimes. Would it also give them some glimpse into their country's history?

It was late and dark when we arrived back in Lijiang. We had

kept our rooms as we had had no clue as to when we would
return, and I was grateful to fall into its familiarity. A hot shower
and herbal tea cleared the troubles of over eight hours of bum-
jumping travelling, but once I lay between the crisp white sheets,
sleep kept at bay. My thoughts were racing, my head filled with
images of a bygone existence. As morning approached, gratitude swept over me as I remembered that today was going to be
a quiet one in this charming little town.

Chapter 7

Tiger Leaping Gorge

Mountains and Memories

The day had started early, unlike the one before when everyone had needed a lie-in after our marathon trip to the past. After storing the bulk of our luggage – which now included several wooden pictures, haggled over for a considerable time – in a small cupboard at the hotel, we took a short taxi trip to the bus station. Giles was able to make himself understood at the ticket office, which enabled us to board a minibus with other western tourists and some locals, one clutching a small baby, others, large canvas bags of things just bought or for sale. We were on our way to Giles and Yoshi's favourite place in the world (not that they've been everywhere, but not far off, at least in this region).

My stomach was complaining from two weeks of different food, eaten at differing times as compared to our fairly strict schedule at home, and I trusted that I would make it to wherever we were going, in time. I hadn't asked the children about the state of their insides, not wanting to give them any ideas that there could be cause for concern. The countryside passed before our eyes, and soon it was apparent that these routes had more than designated stops, as a woman flagged us down. The seats were already full, and she crouched in the doorway at my

feet. Before long, she had climbed over the gearbox and was sitting next to the driver, stroking his face. The road was narrow
and winding, and I trusted that his concentration would remain
with that external extremity and not his own. People flashed
by at the side of the road, many looking like farm labourers on
the way to their fields. We seemed far from civilization, but several were speaking into mobile phones. The journey took longer
than Giles had anticipated, but finally we emerged into an area
of mountains, where we got off the bus. Backpacks in place, we
were ready for another adventure.

Our first stop was Jane's Guesthouse, owned and run by a
fluent English speaker who served food and offered communal
rooms for sleeping. I tried not to imagine the number of bed
bugs within the mattresses as I witnessed how many foreign
bodies must have used these rooms from the signatures that
adorned the walls. I needed a restroom, and it was advisable in
those circumstances to keep that euphemism in mind, otherwise
it would have been impossible to endure. Yoshi came with me
and held the door closed from the outside as this was a one-
for-all situation, and I couldn't crouch and hold the door at the
same time. Two visits later, I felt a little more settled, and some
hot porridge had helped us all feel ready for the next part of this
trip.

Our hostess had an unusual face that fascinated me, and I
wondered if she had some Tibetan blood, or maybe came from
a local ethnic tribe. She ordered us a taxi, and we hopped into a
small minibus. The road took us along the mountainside, some
parts recently prepared, others seeming more like goat tracks.
The mighty Jinsha Jiang River, better known to you and me
as the Yangtze, flowed below us – much farther below than I
would have wished. Just through a tunnel that had been carved
into the face of the rock, we stopped and exited. The roaring of
the water was the first sensation to greet our senses; the next was
the sheer drop from road to river as we saw a group of tourists

on a rock promontory far beneath us. They were specks in the valley, and we could only imagine the sound of the rushing, foaming water in their ears.

Having made use of our video and digital cameras, we clambered aboard what would have been our donkey in days of yore, and continued our speed-thrill, hair-bending journey. The last part was winding and uphill, until we emerged into bright sunshine at the front of a large, modern building. This was another guesthouse named after an English-speaking woman, Tina, supposedly to make us feel less like we had just arrived at the end of the world.

We were shown to a new block of rooms and given two on the second floor, dust covering the surfaces of the brand-new furniture and sticky tape still adorning the toilet seats. Our rooms, which were side by side, had inadequate heating for the cold nights, but the bedding covering the brand-new mattresses was new, crisp, and white, so there were no bed bugs here – yet.

The view from our window was indescribable, a rugged mountainside which changed as the light flickered and moved from one outcrop to the next. This was a new experience for me and also for the children, who had lived their whole lives in Finland, one of the pancakes of the world. How do you describe such natural beauty? Majestic, breathtaking, belittling, awesome? I had no desire to climb them, but have an eye-feast? Yes, please.

After lunch, which had been chosen from a roll-up bamboo menu, the younger members of our party decided to go exploring and left for an easy hike. I needed a rest, both physically and mentally, so returned to the room I was sharing with the children. As I approached it, I looked back in the direction my companions had taken and spied them on the far horizon, about to take a turn out of my sight. Camera in hand, zoom activated, I snapped them just before they disappeared out of view to continue their lives without me. A shower was also necessary. That took some time as I tried to discover how it worked. A power failure in the middle of my investigations didn't help matters, but I got there in the end.

The children enjoyed their walk and decided to accompany Giles and Yoshi the following day, New Year's Eve, on a much more exacting trek up the mountains behind the guesthouse. I knew that I wouldn't make it; anyway, I wanted to end the year in peace and contemplation. What a place to achieve that goal.

Knowing that my offspring would be gone for most of the day, I tried not to think of what they would be facing, or more likely, not facing, on their chosen trek. When I saw their photos later, I also realised that my imagination wouldn't have been that far off even if I had let it run wild, as I saw them standing on ledges or outcrops which seemed to drop from their toes.

After their departure, I tidied our room and made my way to the garden that looked over to the mountains. Flowers were in bloom and greenery around, and I decided to put my thoughts on paper.

31 December 2006 11.20 a.m.

I'm sitting at the guesthouse at Tiger Leaping Gorge, mountains in front of me, their rugged tops shrouded in mist. It's an overcast day, unlike yesterday when we arrived in the blazing sunshine, and even Yoshi said she was too hot! I'm amazed at the majesty of nature – its strength, power, and endurance. How small I feel, a speck in the universe, similar feelings as I had at the Great Wall just a week ago.

A tiny white dog arrives at my side. We have seen many like this in Yunnan, and Tamara made friends with some similar Pekingese-looking dogs along the cobbled streets of Lijiang on our touristy-shopping trips and also in Lanping. This specimen is asking to be stroked, needing a sign of acknowledgment. She reminds me of our dependence on the natural world, not just for what materials it offers, but also for its companionship.

We are two individuals alone, sharing a tiny moment in time. There is no camera to point and click, trying to preserve what cannot be captured. We are two mothers, and I wonder if she is also thinking of her young? Four of mine are now climbing the mountains behind me – trekking, exploring, and discovering themselves. My firstborn was unable to share this time with us. I feel sad about that, and disappointment fills my heart. The sun appears between two peaks, warming my face and reminding me that the light is never far away.

Two red lorries shatter the peace on the bending road below me. Their horns blare and remind me that man has an insatiable need to develop – is that improvement?

Another year is soon to end, one that started in despair and loneliness. Mild medication, a friendly psychologist, and fifty-two weeks later, have I conquered my fears of inadequacy and irrelevance? The sun has gone, covered again by clouds, allowing the mountain breeze to chill my legs and feet. So much like life – the ups and downs, turns and tunnels, and peace and discord.

My companion's fur is soft and comforting. It is now 11.50, and a small bus passes on the road; more people are coming and going – from where, to where? She curls up beside me on the greenery of the raised flowerbeds. I cannot see or hear a soul, only the gushing of the river in the gorge below me. The sun shines again, its warmth absorbed by my dark trousers. Cling to these moments; keep them as a reminder that all things change – constantly. Nothing, good or bad, can be preserved.

I hear the voices of the young women who work here, who sing as they go about their chores, clearing rooms of one-night visitors and preparing food. Their feet clatter on the stairs as they are kept busy with their everyday lives while I live an adventure. What would they think of our still lake and tall trees at home? The endless flatness? Would they miss the vastness of this wilderness?

A young woman rushes to the edge of the precipice where

I am sitting and calls down to someone on the road. Her voice sounds too loud in this experience. A cyclist struggles up the steep road below and to my left. Bright red panniers adorn the rear wheels of his bike. He disappears behind the bend and emerges within seconds onto the road leading to the guesthouse. As I have been writing, my gaze has missed a companion. I see two bikes slow to a halt. More people want to taste the glory and solitude of this place. But for how long will it be like this? Will this unspoilt area be able to maintain its simplicity?

A minibus of well-dressed Chinese tourists arrives, exploding onto the scene. They scream to the mountains, presumably hoping for an echo and disturb my mother-companion sleeping warmly on my lap. Their menu arrives, and my peace has gone. I have no right to it anyway while millions of other souls live daily in noise and confusion. Gratitude pours over me for this flash of remoteness, given me to contemplate.

I phone Arto, who is at home with the cat. He will have just finished his early Sunday morning newspaper delivery in our little town, the front pages no doubt bearing pictures of a noosed ex-Iraqi leader. Another face to this world we have created. That trans-continental link also reminds me of how small we have made our vast planet. Instant communication compared to – what? – three months for my father all those years ago? Maybe I needed to call to remind myself that this is not my reality, merely an oasis, a taste of otherness, in order to live in the real.

My furry bundle returns. We need each other and stare into each other's eyes. No one has spoken to us or asked us what we are doing. We are just allowed to be. To sit. To write. To wonder. Laughter fills the air as the Chinese group share a joke and their lives. A distant American voice floats on the air but remains faceless. Have we all come here to find something, to make sense of our lives?

Some piped music commences, a mixture of Chinese pop

with a flavour of the old. The American voice appears behind me, and cooking smells invade the mountain air. I look at the peaks, stroke my friend, and decide to complete the filling up of my senses.

'A coffee, please. You can bill it to Room 301.'

Their return was welcome, as I only needed a certain length of time for reflection. On our return home, Thomas told me that this was the highlight of the trip for him. It had been hard going, hot, and at times difficult for Tamara's short legs to continue, but the sight of wild horses had revived her. Somewhere in that towering wilderness, a family had set up a diner, offering refreshments for weary travellers. How they got their supplies was a mystery to me, as I saw on the camera the tiny ledges that my family had traversed.

We had a meal together and spent some time playing cards, me taking longer than anyone else to learn the rules as I went along. The New Year started for a group of Australians several hours before it did for the Chinese as we noted when a loud cheer filled the air. We retired to our rooms and snuggled together under the covers to watch a show from Kunming, the capital of this province. It was overly elaborate, taking into consideration that the true local New Year was more than a month away.

After quiet 'Happy New Years' and 'Good Nights', we started 2007, six hours earlier than Arto at home. The next day it was time to say our farewells to these peaks and vales as we boarded another van that had been ordered by the guesthouse. My underarms were red raw like the backs of my legs. Nights had been cold, and I had worn a pink fluffy jumper instead of my pyjamas one night and hadn't taken it off the next day. The sleeves were too tight, and now I was paying for it. We wended our way down the track until we re-entered the trappings of civilisation, where we waited for a public bus. It was basic, and the petrol tank appeared to be above ground behind the driver's seat. This appraisal was confirmed when, partway into our journey back to Lijiang, we stopped at a small fruit stall off the roadside, and a hosepipe was poked through a now-opened window and aimed in the hole, which had been revealed with the removal of the screw cap. Petrol fumes filled the air as the tank was satiated. Oblivious to danger, the driver smoked contentedly as he returned the top and covered it with an old rag – to catch any drips, it can be assumed.

We passed rice paddies, open fields, and houses with tiled roofs, all pointing upwards at the corners. I clicked away and was surprised later at how clear the photos emerged despite the movement of our vehicle. One astounded me as I saw, in the forefront, a farmer and his wife looking like an advert for Mao's latest fashion because I knew that I had not noticed they were further along the road as I took my shot.

Halfway through the journey, a woman took over the controls. She was skilled in driving these winding roads, which climbed, then suddenly tumbled round the next bend. Her mobile phone rang. She answered it and drove for many miles with the phone to her ear, one hand on the steering wheel. I tried not to think about the situation.

Lijiang appeared in stages as we passed modern buildings and ancient ones, every view a glimpse of the uncertainties of this most populous country on earth, fast joining those nations in which the disparity between rich and poor is broadening beyond the bounds of commonsense.

Our old rooms in the hotel were still available. We collected our belongings from storage and settled back into this life. One more day, and we would be returning to the vast metropolis on the east coast which Giles and Yoshi called home. They had to decide shortly whether to continue with another two-year contract.

We wandered to the new part of town and found an area with an artificial stream but genuine trees. Development was in progress, and the town seemed to be expanding towards the mountains. On returning to the old area, we found an online café, although the connection was at a snail's pace because there had been an earthquake off Taiwan. Their menu was a wonder of the English language.

The hot pepper fries the beef
The temple protects the Chicken cube
The water boils the rabbit
Braise in soy sauce the fatty intestine

Unfortunately, or otherwise, I cannot tell you what any of them tasted like. Timo ordered *3 balls of ice cream* and received three oblongs of different colours on a bed of lettuce.

We needed to ascend an almost vertical ladder-like staircase to reach another café, and we found that it hired mountain bikes and equipment. The children tried to use the Internet again, and I had a coffee and watched the world go by beneath me in one of the town squares. I found a photo book about Yunnan and a picture of my reigning monarch with the caption, *Her Majesty Elizabeth 2nd, King of the Great Britain, on a visit to Yunnan nationality College.*

Just hours before we left, we did some last minute shopping in the warmth and light of the winter sun and watched two circles of Naxi matriarchs do a slow dance in one of the town's squares. Their wrinkled skin glowed in the rays, and I wondered what they were thinking about all the gawking tourists. Were they paid for this show of tradition? The non-Chinese residents among us were feeling rather queasy, especially Timo, whose pale, north European skin looked even more translucent than usual.

As we had to vacate the hotel before we needed to travel to

the airport, we spent some time in the main square sitting on the low walls watching the tourists and locals, including several people practising their calligraphy on the ground with huge brushes dipped in water; such beauty disappeared with the heat of the sun. Vendors, who pulled jewellery and other knick-knacks out of their pockets and did not seem to understand the equivalent of 'not interested' in body language, constantly accosted us. It was almost a relief when it was time to hail two taxis for the half-hour trip to the plane. By this time, Timo was doubled up, and I wondered how he was going to manage a five-hour flight. I found it hard to see the children's flight-food wasted – they couldn't even manage their western-looking bread rolls.

Chapter 8

Shanghai Return

Phones and Farewells

It was late when we arrived back in the flat, and everyone was tired. In the early hours, I heard noises that I wished I couldn't. Timo had not been able to get out of bed quickly enough and had deposited the contents of his stomach onto the cotton carpet at his side. What now? I tried to mop it up with toilet paper, but I soon realised that this mishap needed a more concerted effort. Dragging the colourful rug into the bathroom, I washed it as best I could in the circumstances and returned it to our room and draped it over my suitcase that would need packing, yet again, in fewer hours than I could think about at that moment. I felt grateful that there were no fitted carpets.

There was still some money left in the kitty that we had established. Someone suggested that the children could buy new mobile phones; Thomas would be able to get a newer model and Timo and Tamara cease to share one. They would be the last children in their classes to have their own modern toy. We set off to check the merchandise. What a morning! One huge building was full of small stalls selling every make of phone invented by man. Nokia was popular, and for those of you who still think that sounds as though it is a Japanese company, it's Finnish. Christmas decorations still adorned signs and sellers.

Many vendors were asked what kind of deal they could offer on three purchases and finally, much to my relief, someone produced the magic amount out of a hat.

We also did some more window-shopping in the markets, and Yoshi and I went into a small stall manned by a middle-aged couple. He was happy to use his English and seemed knowledgeable about Finland. 'Oh, the country with many lakes and trees.' Yoshi took a photo of them with me, and I promised to send them a copy, whereupon he gave me his business card. Several months after my return home, I attempted to send the digital picture to China, but my emails were returned several times. I made a paper copy and sent it by post, the old-fashioned way. The reply I received some time later was written in neat handwriting and near-perfect English. Both attributes would have been high scorers with my English teachers in school days. 'We've received the letter and photos sent by you. Thank you very much. When the photo was taken at our shop, my wife and I just thought it was a friendly form but didn't think we would get it. Yet it was sent by e-mail many times and at last sent by snail-mail and reached us. — This photo is very precious for us because it came from a foreign country covering a distance of thousands of miles. We regard it as the symbol of the friendship of our two peoples.— '

Enclosed with the letter were some embroidered decorations, which I gave to the teachers of English in my hometown as we had a get-together that same evening to see the photos of my trip. The post office had done a remarkable job.

On our last evening in Shanghai, we went to the Jing Mao Tower, 420.5 metres high, the fourth tallest in the world at the time. Floor eighty-eight was for viewing, outwards and downwards, although the latter was in the middle of the structure, and the view was through glass, which was dizzying enough, especially for those with unsettled stomachs. The views in all directions showed lights like sparkling fairies on various skyscrapers, while others attempting to beat them for the tallest spot were dotted with worker ants that seemed to cling to their work stations like insects with suckered feet.

The river far below was flecked with slow-moving boats, their outlines created by more luminous orbs. The lift descent, as smooth as silk, was accomplished in less time than it's taking me to type about it. We returned to the flat, and I packed our bags, now full of clothes, presents, and souvenirs, for the last time. Our spending had brought us up to the weight we were allowed, although all our hand-luggage-backpacks were heavier than they looked. Next morning, we had another last – taxi rides to the airport followed by checking-in and a tearful, on my part, goodbye to Giles, who had accompanied us to this contemporary construction which receives and sends bodies all around the world. We had been unable to choose our seats on the Finnair web pages as we had done for the outward journey, but discovered that we must be some of the first to check in as we received four seats in a row, in the centre of the plane, as we had had for the outward journey. There would be no disturbing others to go to the toilet and no one disturbing us, apart from ourselves. I managed to eat some of the food that was served, but the children were all complaining of funny tummies and were not even interested in the music that could have kept them entertained through the headphones.

Helsinki Airport seemed very small, but familiar. We found our way to a far extremity where the domestic flights pursue their business and settled in for a five-hour wait. By the time we left the capital at eight p.m., it was two in the following morning for us. Arto was waiting for us in Tampere, our trailer hitched to the back of the car. Going out, our luggage had only just fitted in the boot, and we now had many things 'Made in China'.

Chapter 9

Home Countries

Photos and Facts

We had just completed a round trip of over 25,000 kilometres, on average travelling more than 1,000 per day, and our bodies were shrieking with complaint. It took more than forty-eight hours to get back to Finnish time, although the children had less than that before they returned to school. They had missed several days of classes both ends of our trip, and I trusted that they would all soon catch up with their studies. I sorted through all the presents and bagged them up, ready for different sets of people – Arto's relatives, our friends in the environs of our town, many for England, and some for Australia.

Accompanying these latter two categories, I wanted my family to have photos and videos of our trip. In Lijiang, we had put all the pictures from Giles's and our cameras onto CDs, and back in Shanghai, we had done the same, resulting in us having one set of all the pictures that had been taken. Downloading, sorting, and deciding to discard some of the hundreds of photos from these discs was my job, meaning I had some control over it, but Thomas was in charge of the videos, and it took many requests and pleadings for those to be edited and ready for my April trip to England. I decided to make an album for each of my siblings and one for my eldest son about our trip to Lanping.

For us, I wanted all the photos, but narrowed it down to about six hundred! When I was ready to order, it was a relief to find that the online company had a half-price offer.

My luggage full of my memories, I set off for our hometown in southern England to stay with one of my brothers, Paul, and his wife, Ruth. On the first day, which I had given myself to acclimatise to the British climate and ways, we went to Windsor, my birthplace. It was a sunny day and spring-like. I could have cried. The following day, we were joined by more relatives travelling from all directions. The first to arrive was my eldest son, Ben, with his wife, Kaley, and daughter, Holly. The four of us took some pots of pansies, bought the day before in Windsor, and one of the flowers that my father had grown in our childhood garden to plant on the grave he shared with my mother. Silently, I told him about 'meeting' him in Lanping and that now I wanted to share some of my thoughts and feelings about the country he had loved with some of his other children and their families.

During the previous month, I had shown groups of my English Conversation students in the area of my Finnish hometown a slide show of over three hundred photos, a condensed version of three weeks visiting Shanghai, our Plan village, Xian, Beijing, Lijiang, Lanping, and Tiger Leaping Gorge – twenty-one days of adventure and eye-opening experiences. I had brought the same compilation with me, and using a machine brought by Ben, we managed to show them on the wall, not as clear as they could have been because of the sun shining outside. I had been nervous during the morning wondering whether this assembled group of people would think I was making an unnecessary fuss, gathering them all together for a slide show and buffet meal. We ran out of time to watch all the videos that Thomas had filmed and edited – his first attempt at such a task. Even though it had been left to the last moment, he and I had still had time to add some instrumental Chinese music as background from a CD that I had bought in Lijiang, while the store was playing songs from a Finnish group called *Nightwish* inside the shop and out to the marketplace. I imagine the amateurish filming was slightly boring, but I had asked him to record us bumping up and down in the minibus to Lanping to show what kind of a ride it had been, but I doubt if anyone watching could have picked up on the hidden excitement permeating the vehicle, of not knowing where we were going and whether we would find what we were looking for once we got there.

As we had done no shopping in Lanping itself, I had bought souvenirs in Lijiang for my family, including various locally-made handicrafts, some CDs of Yunnan music, and some videos of traditional dancing. They weren't from the right town, but at least they had come from the same province. My students had only received a sandalwood bookmark each, bought in Xian. We had received our purchases in pastel-coloured woven bags. I filled one for each family and presented it to the member who had the most direct relationship to me. I couldn't help remembering my short conversation with Giles.

'I'm doing this for the others as well.'

'Are you sure they want you to?'

I hadn't been sure then, but was I now? As some of us tried not to let our eyes water, I thought perhaps I was.

⁊∾໑

During these proceedings, John, the eldest sibling present, had returned home to find some old photo albums and a book called *China Call*, written by a cousin, Robert Bolton, about his father, the maternal uncle of my older siblings. When I read it later, I learnt more about their mother's early life. There was also an A5-size tattered notebook filled with messages from American servicemen who had been given refuge by Harry, with notes in his handwriting as to the dates they had stayed and what they had been provided with on their departure. It was vaguely familiar to me, but remembered only through childish eyes. Now it sparkled with possibilities of making sense out of things unremembered, but now discovered. The puzzle would never be completed, but I could attempt to make it recognisable.

At some point during the afternoon, I brought up the subject of Harry having returned to Yunnan in 1949, as told to us by Mr Li. I can remember wanting someone to have heard even the tiniest whisper about it, but no one had. Faith told us that she had Harry's passport, and that seemed the most appropriate place to find confirmation. I spent the next few days with her, but the book of travels wasn't where it should have been and not in the next ten possible places. Was I not meant to know? Does life require that some things remain mysteries?

One of my sisters-in-law, Ruth, had found an old magazine, *The Messenger*, from our childhood church. It was the first edition from January and February 1960, in which my mother, Elsie, had written about her life, and how it had not gone as she had planned. It was introduced with these words, 'A former assistant Matron, now one of our members, tells her story.' So much that afternoon had been about Harry that I felt pleased to hear her words read aloud – not the right voice, but the same heart.

—When I was fifteen years of age I listened to a missionary address, which gave me a strong desire to train as a nurse, with the idea of eventually doing medical missionary work. I began my training at a large hospital in Leeds when I was twenty years old — Eighteen months after beginning my training, I had to leave nursing because of skin trouble. I felt bewildered at God's leading, but after six months I was able to return to training, this time in a London hospital; and although it took me seven years to complete my training, I believe God's hand was in it all — Through the years, the desire to do medical missionary work remained with me, but that door did not open to me. Instead, I married a missionary ten years ago and since then my mission field has been the home.—

As she had written that piece, I'm sure she hadn't planned on being a widow six months later. Ruth's voice came to a halt, and I trust that we all felt a sense of gratitude for the nurturing that Elsie gave us, whether born from her body or not. Whoever said that blood is thicker than water never met our mum.

It was fascinating reading the notebook and looking through all the photos at Faith's during the following days. I had quite a pile of albums to sift through, as Faith had also found some, including one that had belonged to our sister, Ivy, who had died in 1986. The new information I gleaned was enlightening, and, although the trip to China would have made more sense with the facts now at my fingertips, I felt that the pioneering aspect had been far more relevant to understanding, in however small a way, the journeys that my father had taken, both physically and emotionally.

One of my discoveries, which the older ones must have known but hadn't realised that I didn't, was that their mother had gone to China in 1923 at the age of twenty-two. Her brother Leonard and his wife, Olive, followed a little later. They had worked, along with other missionaries, in Yunnan Province, mainly around Kunming and Wei Hsi, a town further west and closer to Tibet. At one point, some of them had made a pioneering trip south and found themselves near the Burmese border in a place called Lanping. Len and Victoria's father founded the Tibetan Border Mission to support his children's missionary endeavours. Vic had gone home to England for a holiday in

1928 and met Harry, who had already felt that he should go to China. They married in September of that year and travelled together in November on the *Empress of France* to Hong Kong, via Singapore, as far as I can make out from some of the photos and their captions.

Shades of brown depicted another world in the photos, most showing their age. Travelling by mule and on foot, coolies carried their large packs of belongings on their backs. Were they glad to have work, but wondering why these foreigners wanted to face all the hardships that such journeys encompassed? Once I got to the pictures of the couple's shared life in Lanping, it dawned on me why we had been taken to the second set of derelict buildings and why Alfred and Martin had been struck by them. How stupid I had been. Where had I thought Harry lived before he built the house that had claimed my heart? Truth be told, I hadn't thought about it, but here it was. Photo captions jumped from the pages. 'Our landlord'. 'Our wing of the house'. This was one of life's 'of course' moments. On their first arrival, they had had to find somewhere to rent, and that was where Alfred had been born in 1930, and Dorothy two years later. She had died at sixteen months, half a year before the birth of Ivy in December 1933, possibly also in those buildings they called home. Which year they built their own home was still an unknown, but at least I could now put that second compound of now-wood-storage buildings in a Harry context.

One of the photos took my breath away as I looked down on the building that had captured me, but from a vantage point that we had never viewed it. It stood all on its own – no walls surrounding it, no extra rooms on a raised platform, no fortifications. The area where we had eaten strawberries was a vegetable garden, and the pear trees were in evidence, standing guard each side of the front door. Now I could imagine my father and his family in their true setting, not one changed by seventy years of history.

So many aspects of their lives were recorded in the prints, which Harry had developed in his own darkroom. There were photos of journeys they had taken with the children carried on bamboo stretchers, market days, buying lime and Tibetan butter, them digging a well and eating a meal in the garden, helpers carrying water for drinking and for watering the garden, and people crossing the Mekong River by a bamboo rope bridge. Ordinary and extraordinary moments captured and fixed in albums. How many stories do these scenes conceal behind their shiny facades?

Not wanting to trust these priceless papers to the plane's hold, I put them all in my hand luggage. The checker at the x-ray machine took a long time staring before he asked his colleague to check what I had. The albums were so dense that he had been unable to see a thing. Everything was emptied out, including the contents of my handbag, which had been inside the larger one. I knew that I had nothing to hide, or even be ashamed of, but it was unnerving all the same.

The following weeks were a frenzy of activity as I scanned all the photos into our computer. Each page of every album had to be placed carefully beneath the cover of the scanner and held there because of the thickness involved. There was also the notebook, which, along with the hand-written entries, held glued-in letters to and from American officials, some sheets of paper so flimsy that they looked as though they would disintegrate at the gentlest touch. As I turned each page and read the names of the Americans, I began to wonder whether any of these men were still alive. If they had been as young as twenty at the time, that would put them in their eighties now.

A famous site had an unexpected influx of searches for the next weeks as I entered names – *Barnard, Cole, Jones, King, Marshall, Yee ...* – and places that had been given as home addresses – *Alabama, California, Missouri, New York, Oregon ...* – and squadrons, and any piece of information that might lead me to a living person. *30th Transport Group, 77th Transport Squadron, 308th Bomb Group* ... some seemed promising, and then one piece of information wouldn't fit. I saved lots of data – when the men had joined the armed services, where, and what family, if any, they had had – but nothing led to an existing email address. What had I expected?

I found many web pages dedicated to the China-Burma-India (CBI) war, apparently forgotten by the world at large, but remembered by friends and relatives of those who had served – and died – in that arena. I scoured page after page of details hunting for my father's name or any of the men who had passed through Lanping, but without success. I did find a reference to another missionary who had helped in a similar fashion and felt such disappointment that the person recording his time there had not been in Lanping.

Not having thought about computer ergonomics, I began to experience an intense pain in my right shoulder, which spread down my arm until my forearm was so heavy, I could hardly lift it. When my thumb and next two fingers went numb, I decided I had better take action. After various rounds of physiotherapy over the next several weeks, the feeling began to return. Only after my recovery did I comprehend how intense had been my longing to find someone who had known Dad, who could give me some first-hand description of how he had talked, what he had done, who he had been.

I did manage to find on the *Find My Past* website copies of the pages of the ship's log showing Vic's spinster voyage, where she had been travelling as a missionary. It was interesting to see that when Harry accompanied her five years later, he had gained that title, and she was a housewife. There was also a record of the February 1935 family trip back to China via Bombay on the *Strathnaver*, which was bound for Brisbane. Alfred had been almost five, Ivy only one, and this trip had followed the one to England when Harry had received the hymnbook.

Then inspiration struck. Why not make a presentation of Harry's life using the photos and information I had now obtained? Thomas got the engine started, and the fun followed as I took the reins. Choosing which photos to include was the hardest part because there were so many, and they had not been catalogued in chronological order. I decided to make it as time-friendly as possible, but with themes running throughout, such as journeys into neighbouring villages and hamlets, local activities, like gardening and shopping, and the building of the Church Hall. Cutting, pasting, editing, finding a suitable background, and the constant dilemma of whether to create text or use original photo captions ensued. Sometimes the photos wouldn't stay where I wanted them to, or the text overlapped the picture or wouldn't show. Each slide became a minor miracle.

Chapter 10

History Comes Alive

Ancestors and Americans

In 2005, I became interested in finding out more about my ancestors and joined *Genes Reunited*. Through that site, I had made contact in May 2006 with an unknown paternal relative, Dave, the son of one of my also unheard-of cousins. He filled me in on some details about people I had had no knowledge of and regaled me with his only memory of Harry. 'From memory, I only met your dad once; it must have been about 1954, and he had just come back from China, and I was expecting him to be using chopsticks! So I asked the question, and he got his pen and pencil (blue and green) and ate the rest of the meal, which must have impressed me as that is all I can remember.' He didn't quite have it right about how long Harry had been back in the west, but the tale about the chopsticks showed me that my father must have had a sense of humour and a good imagination.

Several months later, in September, another second cousin and I found each other via the same channels. Her mother is thirty-three years older than me and is my cousin. The generations of my family have always seemed rather confused in my mind. I have done nothing to help that, with my own children's births spanning twenty years so that I have a daughter

and granddaughter only eight years apart, the former being the
elder, I'm pleased to say.

Angela and I have corresponded since that time, and she has
helped me a great deal in discovering my roots, for which I
am grateful. In November of the same year, she sent me two
photos of my grandparents, Samuel and Mary. By that time, I
had found them on various censuses, but had no idea what they
had looked like. It was strange to see one's closest forebears for
the first time, although as it happened, it wasn't. 'They didn't
look familiar at all, so I was pretty sure that I hadn't seen them
before. However, I've been sorting out the few old photos I
have and found one of a group with my dad and his first wife,
Victoria. It must have been taken on a trip home at some point.
And there, sitting next to Dad, are his parents!'

Before Angela had sent me the photos, I had had no idea
that those two figures were my grandparents. Since then she has
sent me various certificates that she has discovered of our joint
ancestry, and Faith and I were able to meet her in April 2007
when I visited England with all my Chinese treasures. The following month I received one of the most precious emails I have
ever opened. Attached was a sepia photo taken in 1909, when
Harry was about fourteen, of his whole family – parents and
siblings – posed in their garden. Before that, the earliest photo
I had seen of my father had been taken in 1925 when he was
thirty years of age.

Another special offer at the developers enabled me to make
large copies of this photo for all my family, which I took to
England that summer along with the presentation of 'Harry's
Life' on CDs. There was also a transcription of the notebook,
which had taken an age to type as most pages were handwritten,
and could have been mistaken for doctors' prescriptions, so
illegible were some of the greetings and signatures. The letters and lists that had been glued in were not in chronological
order, so I also attempted to put that right within the transcript,

and some kind of story emerged, with the servicemen's entries coinciding with correspondence from their higher officers. Each entry had been someone's life, and I wished that a larger chunk of mine had been spent investigating them.

One photo that had been part of my childhood was of my father just before he died in 1960, standing in front of our front door with two Americans dressed in civvies. I knew that they had been connected with Harry in some way in China, and the name of one of them, Morris Kaplan, had stuck in my memory. Before I set out for China, I had tried finding material on the Internet to do with him and my father, as well as Harry's name linked with Lanping. I tried all kinds of combinations, but nothing had materialised. Then, unexpectedly, one of my nephews, Chris, found an article online about the paralysed American whom my father had kept alive until he could be evacuated. This story was a legend in our family, but I had never known the details. Here it was, compiled from information given by those involved. I was excited, although I couldn't fathom why I had not found it myself. The article had been written in 1996 in *Air Force Magazine*, the online journal of the Air Force Association, and was entitled 'Valor: All for One'.

As commander of the 803rd Air Evacuation Squadron, based in northeast India, flight surgeon Maj. Morris Kaplan was responsible for air evacuation throughout the China-Burma-India theater. In the summer of 1944, he was informed that an American lieutenant, a member of a mapping party in a remote area of southwest China, was at a Christian mission in Lanping directed by British cleric Rev. Harry Fisher. The lieutenant was suffering from acute polio and needed to be evacuated. Major Kaplan knew this was an urgent mission that he must lead himself. He immediately flew over the Hump to Kunming, where he learned there was no landing area in the mountainous terrain near Lanping, more than 200 miles northwest of Kunming.

Against the advice of old hands, Major Kaplan insisted on being flown to Lanping, where he would bail out with his medical supplies. Twice, the flight was turned back by violent weather, with no forecast of immediate improvement. Major Kaplan then set out in a jeep with three companions on the five-day trip to Lanping. When the road became impassable, the mayor of a small village agreed to store the jeep and provide horses and an armed guard to get them through bandit-controlled territory. Once beyond that, the guards departed with the horses, leaving Major Kaplan and his men to finish the last 25 difficult miles to Lanping on foot. At the mission, they found 6-foot-3-inch Lt. Robert Wesselhoeft totally paralyzed, being kept alive with artificial respiration administered by a team of Chinese peasants Reverend Fisher had recruited. Major Kaplan's problems seemed insurmountable. The Lieutenant could not be carried the 75 miles to the jeep while manual respiration was continued. They needed a mechanical respirator and an airplane to transport Wesselhoeft.

Major Kaplan and his companions built the mechanical respirator using two boards hinged on one side at a separation slightly less than the thickness of Wesselhoeft's chest. A handle was attached to the upper board. By pressing on the handle, air was pushed from Wesselhoeft's lungs. As the pressure was released, fresh air flowed in.

Now, where to land an airplane at Lanping? The rescuers finally found a small flat island in the Lanping River, but it was covered with stones, small boulders, and vegetation. That problem was solved by the local warlord - with whom Reverend Fisher had a good relationship - who rounded up 200 Chinese laborers to clear a runway where a skillful pilot could land an L-5. This took three days. The next day an L-5 from Kunming touched down, flown by gung ho pilot Maj. Freddy Welsh, who had volunteered.

Everything that could be removed from the L-5 was discarded so that Lieutenant Wesselhoeft could be laid on his back with his head just behind and to the left of the pilot's seat. Some changes to the respirator also were made, among them a handle that Major Welsh could operate every 25 seconds with his left hand while flying the plane with his right. The Lieutenant and his respirator were laboriously fitted into the available space.

Freddy Welsh had to abort his first takeoff but succeeded on a second attempt. He later described the circuitous three-hour flight to Kunming: "I finally gained enough altitude to clear a 9,300-foot ridge … into the worst weather I have ever flown in. But I did not miss a single stroke with the respirator lever." He ran into torrential rain "such as I had never seen. I became alarmed that the thermal currents would tear the wings off that little plane." At times flying at less than 100-feet altitude for visual navigation, he saw a familiar river and followed it to his base. With the fuel gauge on empty, he landed at Kunming as the engine quit.

Lieutenant Wesselhoeft, a nephew of Massachusetts Sen. Leverett Saltonstall, was flown to Calcutta, placed in an iron lung, then flown to Walter Reed Hospital in Washington, D.C. He remained in an iron lung for a year before recovering enough to leave the hospital in a wheelchair. He later earned a doctorate and taught for several years. He owed his life to many caring people, including the Fisher family, but foremost among them are Morris Kaplan and Freddy Welsh.

Thanks to Capt. Allen Balint for calling this story to our attention and to Colonel Kaplan for providing details.

Forty-seven years after one of the main characters involved in that situation visited our typical English semi near London, I found his entry in the Lanping notebook.

```
Morris Kaplan Maj. Med. Corps
803 Med. Air Evac. Squadron
APO629
12 Corona St.
Denver, Colorado


Mr. Fisher - you and your wonderful family are
among the sweetest people I ever have known. M. K.
```

On the same page was another message.

```
John K. Burns Lt. Col. M.C.
Hq. 14AF c/o Surgeons Office
APO 627 N.Y.C.
2721 So. Post St
Spokane, Wash. U.S.A.


Mr. Fisher is the finest gentleman it has been
my pleasure to meet. He has been extremely helpful
to our American airmen and deserves our highest
respect and thankfulness. J.K.B.
```

I wonder if he was the other visitor who came to my childhood home with Major Kaplan.

The *gung-ho* pilot also made an entry:

```
Fred G. Welsh, Maj. AC  8 July 1944
Hq. 69th Wg 14th U.S.A.A.F.
Glen Head, L.I. New York
West Englewood, New Jersey


Landed airstrip in L-5 to evacuate patient
```

```
(Harry's writing) Arrived July 8th, left July
9th
```

The sick man had been accompanied by the only name in the book that sounded Finnish.

```
John E. Partanen, 1st Lt., A.C.
3rd Photo Mapping Squadron
MacDill Field, Tampa 8, Florida
Ajo, Arizona, U.S.A.

Arrived in Lanping on June 25th with a sick
officer. The efforts of Mr. Fisher on our behalf are
deeply appreciated. I cannot express my gratitude
to him or to his wonderful children.
(Harry's writing) Arrived June 25th, left July
12th
```

He also wrote the entry for the invalid.

```
Robert (NMI) Wesselhoeft, Jr., 2nd Lt., A.C.
3rd Photo Mapping Squadron
552 Gay Street, Westwood, Mass.

Lt. Wesselhoeft was brought here in a critical
condition from 2 days north of Lanping. John E.
Partanen
(Harry's writing) Arrived June 25th, left by
plane July 9th
```

Fifteen days must have seemed like a lifetime for the local Chinese who were pumping that respirator, day and night.

The following letter from the notebook was written several months before the adventure with the paralysed serviceman, and shows that Harry's support had been ongoing.

US Army Forces, Chabua, Assam, India
2 March 1944
Mr. Harry Gladstone Fisher
Tibetan Border Mission
Lanping, Yunnan, S.W.China

Dear Mr. Fisher:

On behalf of Sgt. Beauchamp, his Commanding
Officer, the Rescue Squadron, and all of our Officers
and men of the Army Air Transport Command, whom you
have so generously received in your home, I should
like to express our sincere appreciation, and that
of the Commanding Officer of this Sector. It is an
inspiration to all of our flyers to know as they
do of your kind hospitality to seventeen of their
comrades at various times since November, 1943.
Sgt. Beauchamp is only the most recent to return,
but his gratitude for your kind welcome was shared
by all sixteen who preceded him. You are a charter
member of our Rescue organization.

We are taking steps, even at this moment, to secure
the items which you requested in the letter of which
Beauchamp was bearer. Also at present there are the
equivalent of three jeep-loads of supplies, supposedly to go or on their way to you now overland, which
should shortly be delivered to you at Lanping.

If from time to time you can definitely identify
a plane circling overhead as our Rescue Ship, and
can spell out any of your needs with large white
letters, we shall attend to them with all possible
promptness.

Anything we may be able to do for you, such as
today's dropping of things you'd requested, will be
done most willingly. By comparison with your personal
sacrifices for our flyers, these are little indeed.

Very sincerely yours,
(sig.)
JOHN G. NESBITT
Captain, Air Corps, U.S. Army

It's good to know that the help my family was able to give could be rewarded with material goods that they needed. Life with five children can't have been easy, especially in such an out-of-the-way location.

Harry had also been responsible for locating and burying several bodies of American servicemen who had been killed in the area. Death had certainly become a part of their lives. The following letter is on two sheets of flimsy airmail paper, hand-written and stained with age.

```
Guerrilla School, Yung Lung
April 28, 1944
Missionary Fisher, Lanping, China
Dear Sir:
On behalf of the American Military Forces in
China I wish to thank you for your efforts and
trouble in taking care of the American Airmen killed
in crash of a plane in your vicinity and also such
aid as you have given to survivors who had the good
fortune to "walk out". We, at this station, are
sending you a few items which I am sure you can
use and if you have any specific requests let Cpl.
EVERTSEN know and perhaps we can send up later.
    I regret we cannot send an Officer on this mission
but we are only two and are conducting a military
school here for the Guerrilla Forces. I, there-
fore, am sending Corporal Evertsen to conduct the
bodies back for interment in the American Cemetery
in Poashan. Such (unreadable) give him will be
greatly appreciated. He has instructions to reim-
burse you or others for any expense incurred in
moving and interring the bodies and such expense
in disinterring, and preparing remains for the
return trip. Please advise him as to the best way
to prepare remains for the trip and as mentioned,
he is prepared to pay all expense.
```

Coolies for return trip will be paid on arrival
at Burma Road at Weyo. It is presumed return trip
will be down Mekong through Tsao Kien to Weyo.

If there are any other remains of crashed
American airmen, desire that they also be secured
if possible. The American Army stands ready to
pay suitable reward for location and identification
of American bodies and also in the matter of aid
to American survivors. We would appreciate your
giving publicity, especially to the latter, and
any advice you may give in the latter, in aiding
escaping Americans from Burma territory will also
be appreciated.

Accept the deepest thanks from all Americans.

Yours respectfully,

James M. Carr

Lt. Col. Inf. U.S. Army

Harry wrote the following letter for any American servicemen
who had to bail out in the area where he was living.

Tibetan Border Mission
Lanping, Yunnan, Free China
United States Army Personnel,
Dear Sirs,

You are in a sub district of Lanping, namely
_____ therefore will be brought here, where the
magistrate's residence is situated. From here we
can get in touch by radio with the Rescue Squadron
at Yunnanyi and the Rescue Plane will drop you
your needs within a short period. From here too,
we can get horses and carriers for your journey
either South or East, where a jeep can pick you up
and take you on to Yunnanyi. We have been able to
assist quite a few of your comrades in this way and
have enjoyed the fellowship and their stay in the
home. You are ____ days journey from here and will
be provided with horses and carriers according to

your needs. Please find enclosed a few English-Chinese sentences, which will help you to converse with the local official so as to enable you to arrive here without undue delay. Should you wish to send in a letter to Lanping, ask the local official to send a runner with same, stating Plane's number, date of bailing out, number of men, is Dr. needed and any other particulars you may think useful and I will send same off to Yunnanyi, thus saving perhaps one or two days and also the Rescue Plane a lot of unnecessary searching.

Trusting you all bailed out safely and that you will have a pleasant journey to Lanping,

I remain,

Yours sincerely,

Harry G. Fisher.

These are the sentences that Harry made available – I have only been able to transcribe the English.

Send a search party for the other men.

We want to leave for Lanping tomorrow.

We want (state no.) horses, with saddles. 1 2 3 4 5 6 7 8 9 10

We want carriers (state no.)

We want escort.

We need carriers for injured man or men.

We are hungry and need food. Chicken - Eggs - Vegetables

We want boiling water - A fire - Washing water - Water to wash feet

Has this water boiled? Boiled, Not boiled

Please send a runner at once to Lanping with this letter.

I need a sheet of paper, envelope and pencil.

Please send these people out; we want to go to bed.

```
    Please give us a few sheets of grass paper!!!
(For toilet paper.)
    Please give me some paste to seal up this
letter.
    Please keep this letter here, for others may
need it.
    Can you see that we have no delay en route to
Lanping.
    Many thanks for all your help and kindness during
our stay here.
```

In January 1995, while our family was still living in Helsinki, I tuned into the BBC's *World Service*. I was cooking dinner and watching Timo, then a toddler, playing on the floor, and Tamara, then a three-month-old, sitting in a springy seat at eye-level. The programme I had accidentally tuned into was a music request show called 'Anything Goes'. I could hardly believe my ears when I thought I heard Lanping, Yunnan, China, mentioned as the home of the person asking for the song 'Getting to Know You'. Even though I had three children under four and was heading towards my forty-fourth birthday, and my life already seemed full enough, both physically and emotionally, I decided to write to the BBC to try to make contact with the person – then unknown. Looking back, this was the start of my believing that a connection with China was possible, not necessarily going there, but at least making some link. One month later, by which time I had given up hope of hearing about the matter again, I received a reply. 'Should you wish to send a letter to the listener in Yunnan Province, China, it can be sent here, and we will forward it.'

Looking now at the rough copy of the letter I sent, it took me a further month to work out how to introduce myself and explain my interest in their part of the world. The reply arrived several months later, and had been typed on flimsy airmail paper on 17 May 1995, what would have been Harry's 100th birthday. How special was that?

Tien Yung told me many facts about Lanping County and the town, including that the majority of the population were from the minority groups Bai, Lisu, and Pumi. He also mentioned Lijiang, from where we had travelled to Lanping, although at the time we visited there, I had completely forgotten the name. We have corresponded since then, sporadically, sometimes losing track of each other because of new addresses, both electronic and stationary, but always finding our way back. His choice of song had been prophetic.

He helped me with the translation of a Chinese document from 1924 that I found in one of the photo albums. It was printed on the thinnest paper I have seen, and it must have referred to Victoria's belongings that needed to be paid for before they would be released.

> Imports Release of Teng-yueh Trading Port
> The Teng-yueh Port supervises that, in order for a release to be granted, the merchant priest from —, declares imported goods totalling 40 loads/ baskets of miscellaneous goods/ luggage. In light of Article 9 regarding Yunnan-Burma trade affairs successively discussed by China and U.K. in the 20th year of the reign (AD 1875-1908) of Emperor Guangxu in the Qing Dynasty, imported goods, as stipulated in the customs tariff regulations of trading ports in China, enjoy a tariff reduction of 3/10 (three tenths). The merchant is entitled to a release following a tariff payment of 1.687 liang of silver at an official banking house. With a tariff payment receipt turned in for inspection, the merchant shall, by presenting this release, commence goods transportation. Release issued on November 21st of the 13th Year of The Republic of China (Nov. 21 1924).

He also translated the Chinese characters painted around the doorframe of Mr Li's room. In my pen pal's words, 'The sophisticated version of Chinese characters is no longer used in Chinese mainland. Only old people know how to write them. Despite this, most people here, including me, don't mind reading them.' I think the words must refer to Mr Li's parents and his wife – they make for sad reading.

> *That she/he passed away before seventy years of age tormented her/his offspring.*
>
> *With grief-stricken viscera, the weak child wears tear-stained clothes.*
>
> *A pure heart devoid of rank and fortune returned to originality.*
>
> *Having handled the three funerals, I felt no qualms and lived all by myself.*
>
> *The son clad in mourning dress, wailed in the depth of night.*

In Harry's old notebook, I also learned a little more about the family's escape in 1944.

> 26 September 1944
> Mr. Fisher:
> All arrangements have been made for your trip out. Upon your arrival, my station [will] contact me or Major Gregory. You will be taken anywhere in India you choose. Your baggage will not be limited. Send me a message by Chinese net stating where you want to go and the amount of baggage you will have. If possible give me the date you plan to arrive here. (in handwriting) Best of luck to all.
> (sig.)
> Captain ROLLAND C. BENNETT

A week later, a diligent secretary typed the following sheet:

R E S T R I C T E D
Headquarters
1333 AAF Base Unit
India China Division, Air Transport Command
 Apo #629
3 October 1944
Subject: Travel Orders
To: Commanding Officer, 1338 AAF Base Unit, APO
#488
 (Att: Search and Rescue Officer)

Pursuant to auth contained in 2nd Ind to Ltr,
1338 AAF BU, APO #488, 11 September 1944, Subj: "Air
Transportation for Civilians", the following named
civilian personnel, Tibetan Border Mission, will
proceed o/a 10 October 1944, via first available
military aircraft fr Yunnanyi, China to Calcutta,
India, via Chabua, Assam:

 Mr. Harry G. Fisher
 Mr. Alfred Fisher
 Mr. John Fisher
 Mr. Paul Fisher
 Miss Ivy Fisher
 Miss Faith Fisher

 APR #4-CHU-25883 GR 6 BRI.
 Baggage limitations not to be imposed.

 By order of Lieutenant Colonel JOYCE:

 ELMER W. EARNEST
 Captain, Air Corps

There are several entries in the notebook from servicemen who met the family somewhere on that outward journey.

One of the most outstanding events of my life has been that of making the acquaintance of the Fisher family. "Remarkable" is not adequate to describe them. An added privilege came to me when Major Gregory sent me to accompany them across the "hump". Lt. George and myself made harnesses for the smaller children so that in case of emergency we could jump "two on a chute".

Mr. Fisher has been profuse in expressing his appreciation for what the ATC has done for him and his family, but I should like to say that anything we have done is small repayment for the magnificent work he has done for our crew members who have found it necessary to "bail out" over the "hump".

So to one of the grandest families I have ever met, let me say, "Godspeed and God bless you all."
    Sincerely,
    Vernon O. Rogers, Chaplain (Capt.), U.S. Army Air Corps
    707 Virginia Avenue, Martinsburg, W. Va

I cannot leave their return journey to England without adding a menu that I found among the papers. With all my heart, I hope that my family were given some leftovers – even if they had no idea what the celebration was.

Thanksgiving Dinner
OFFICERS' MESS
23rd November, 1944
INDIA
Fresh Shrimp Cocktail
Roast Goose
Pecan Nut Dressing   Giblet Gravy

```
Mashed Potatoes
Green Peas              Golden Bantan Corn
Lettuce & Tomato Salad
w/Mayonaise

Parkerhouse Rolls
Pumpkin Pie             Vanilla Cake w/Walnut Icing

Assorted Nuts           Candy
Fruit Punch
Coffee
```

Soon after their return to England in January 1945, my father received a letter from Brigadier General Earl S. Hoag, who seems to have been stationed in London at the time.

```
Headquarters
European Division, Air Transport Command
(1400th AAF Base Unit)
APO 741, c/o Postmaster
New York, N.Y.

Office of the Commanding General
18 January 1945

My dear Fisher

The other day I was greatly interested in an
article which appeared in the London Evening News
announcing the return of you and your family.
    You perhaps may not recall, but I was in command
of the India China Division of the Air Transport
Command about a year ago and was quite familiar with
the outstanding service which you were rendering
to that Division. Your cooperation and assistance
to our Air Search and Rescue Unit were outstanding
```

and I know that many of our people owe their lives to the work which you carried on in your outpost.

I trust that you will not fail to let me know should you be in London at any time and that the New Year and many others will give you the rest and relaxation which you have so thoroughly earned.

Again, please accept my thanks for the out-standing service which you have rendered to the Air Transport Command together with my very best wishes.

Sincerely,

(sig.)

EARL S. HOAG

Brigadier General, U.S. Army, Commanding

Mr. Harry G. Fisher
Orchard House
Hindolveston, near Dereham
Norfolk, England

My father replied, quite promptly if I think about his situation, and received an answer dated 17 February 1945, this time addressed to *Mr.* Fisher.

Your very kind letter was waiting for me when I returned from a rather extended trip several days ago.

Thank you so much for the many kind things you have said regarding the Air Transport Command and particularly for the Chinese money, which you enclosed. It was very kind of you to send them to me and I am certainly very pleased to have them.

I hope that you will have an opportunity to get to London soon and that you will contact me when you do.

With kindest regards, I am,

Sincerely,

Earl S. Hoag

I wonder if Harry managed to meet him in London. If he did, it had to have been quite soon after the last letter was written because a few months later, the writer would be in the vicinity of Potsdam where Truman, Churchill, and Stalin held their notorious conference.

Chapter 11

Tentative Tribal Trip

Who and When?

Following my two sojourns in England in April and July of 2007, it seemed that there was some interest among my kin who still resided there in making a family foray to what I had made the focus of our lives. I had shown that Lanping was accessible and possible, and no one was getting any younger. Giles had made a further contract to stay in Shanghai, and he was willing to be our organiser again. Tentatively, I suggested that such an adventure would be achievable and that I could be the link between England and China, the two countries that joined us all together.

Three couples showed some interest, two brothers and one sister. The earliest opportunity would be October, when Giles had some holiday, but that was thought to be too soon, and finally Easter 2008, which would fall in the last half of March, was decided upon.

John, who would be seventy in January, and his wife, Ann, would be the patriarchal couple of the expedition. He had been born in Lanping in 1938 and was not quite seven when he left there for his new life in England. What a journey that must have been, travelling west via India with American help. Paul, the next in age and born in 1939, decided that his health was not good enough, a decision that has been a constant disappointment to the rest of us, and I am sure to him and his wife, Ruth, as well. Faith, the baby of Harry's first family, had been born in 1941 and was only three when they made their escape. John had a few memories, but Faith had none. Our youngest brother, Stephen, also decided to come. He had been only seven when our father died and had fewer memories than I had, but China held some fascination for him. Faith's husband, Mike, and Steve's wife, Jane, completed the group.

So with Giles and Yoshi, there would be four pairs and me, the lone wolf at many of life's moments. The English contingent had to decide how much of the country they wanted to see or whether Lanping would suffice. I have a feeling that it was the younger members who thought they might as well make the most of such an opportunity, especially as they had their own internal travel agent in the form of their nephew.

After Giles gave them several alternatives, they decided to travel to Beijing from London and then fly southwest to Lijiang, as we had done after Christmas 2006. I would first fly to Shanghai and meet them there with Giles and Yoshi. We could spend a day or two acclimatising to the country and each other. Such a gathering of my family had never taken place before, and none of the others had yet met Giles's wife. Then we would hire a bus and driver and translator for Lanping and spend two or three days there. This sounded good to me as I had seen little of the town and surrounding area on my first trip, and it would be good to experience a little more of the place that had held my father's heart. This time we had Mr Li's address and telephone number, so we could warn him of such an invasion.

Giles informed us that we could get a direct flight from Lijiang to Chengdu, home of the panda-breeding programme. I can remember thinking that I had better keep that information to myself, or Tamara would be pestering me to allow her to come again. Maybe selfishly, I wanted this trip to be spent as me

– an adult sister, and the mother of an adult. For me, so much of the previous trip had been concerned with ensuring that the children were happy, and that their bodily functions were working correctly, which had been accomplished for most of the time. After the pandas, we would part company, the England contingent continuing to Xian and Beijing, Giles, Yoshi, and I to Shanghai where I would give myself a day's breather before returning to Finland.

By December, all the plans had been made and international flights booked and paid for. I started filling in a new visa form and discovered that my fee would now be less than for Finns, a move made in reciprocation for fees raised in the other direction. If I'd been American, it would have been three times more. How much had they raised theirs by? The form had been streamlined and included a few health questions that had been asked on the plane last time. This was much more sensible. It would be easier to refuse someone a visa than disembarkation.

Then the bombshell dropped. Mike had been having problems with angina, and their family wasn't sure whether he should undertake such a demanding journey. Faith didn't want to go on her own, and I felt devastated. She had been the main reason that I wanted to make a pilgrimage to Lanping again as she had been instrumental in bringing about Giles and my reunion in 1999, after thirteen years separation. This was the least I could do for her, and when I had phoned her from the old house, Giles had said, 'I'll bring you here, too, one day.' Was that promise about to be shattered?

Mike said that they would make a decision by the time of the whole family's get-together a few days after Christmas. I sat by the computer waiting for the message. The journey would continue without them, but it wouldn't be the same; I knew that somewhere deep down, and my heart ached.

'Could we decide by the end of January?' Another wait. I know that I wondered why they were not trusting more as their faith proclaimed. Not wanting to influence their choice one way or the other, I kept my thoughts to myself, and didn't express the disappointment that was surging through my being.

It was several days into February before the message came that Mike and Faith *would* be coming with us. All was back on track with an unexpected bonus. During the medical deliberations, we had received an email from one of Alfred's eldest twin daughters in Australia saying that she had offered to pay for his international flights if he wanted to come with us. Right from the beginning of the planning, everyone had expressed the wish that Alfred could be a part of our group. Not only had he been back to Lanping in 1997, but he had memories of their lives there as children and also understood and spoke Chinese. We had kept Christine and Katharine informed of our plans – hoping. On seeing our itinerary, Alfred decided that he would like to spend longer in Lanping, rather than visiting the tourist attractions after. He would fly to Beijing, meet the Brits, and they would travel together to Lijiang. This was getting more exciting as we went along. Alfred has been this tall, distant figure for me, more like an unknown father than a brother. He was twenty-one at the time of my birth and already living away from home. Soon after our father's death in 1960, he immigrated to Australia with his German wife. I saw him once after that in the early 1980s. That had been it – a stranger who held memories in his heart that I had never been able to grasp. Now here he was, my eldest brother, able to share those remembrances and repossess his true position as patriarch of our tribe.

But there was more to come – the icing on the cake, the pot of gold at the end of the rainbow. About five days after Faith and Mike's decision to make the journey with us, my eldest son Ben contacted Giles and me by email to ask for our intended itinerary. I read the words over and over, not able to believe my eyes. Did he want to join us as well? When they were young, how many years had I envisaged this scene, my boys and I together, safe and secluded. Was I going to spend time with them as their mother and tiller of ancestral roots?

Could there be any more changes? Yoshi's parents were now living in America, and her maternal grandparents would be celebrating their sixtieth wedding anniversary at the same time as our trip. She decided that she should go to be with them in Colombo. At the final count, we were a group of ten – three couples, three men, and me, ever the odd one.

❦

There are only a few weeks to go now before I leave for China again. It is March 2 today, which would have been my mother Elsie's 96th birthday, and Mother's Day in England this year, and I am contemplating spending some quality time with my eldest children. The thought fills me with wonder and trepidation. So much history has passed between us, as well as passed us by, and my insecurities seem to surface in their company, even though they are in no way responsible for me having those feelings. This will be a momentous meeting as I endeavour to be Mum.

Now British Airways are planning a strike over Easter just at the wrong time for my brothers and sister. Ben is travelling on a Chinese airline to Shanghai and will then travel with Giles and me, returning there when we do. His international flights will not be affected. We are all hoping that the negotiations at BA are resolved.

Through all the planning, I have been keeping John's son Phil, who lives in Spain with his Spanish wife and their three sons, informed of our arrangements. He is unable to come with us, although he and his parents would have liked him to. He teaches English and had prepared a sheet for his students entitled 'Stages of Flying'. He decided to send us all a copy by email, blue text with important vocabulary italicised and red. It was funny in places, but not very reassuring.

Nerves are kicking in now, and not just from reading Phil's encouraging words. This will be a once-in-a-lifetime for all of us, and my emotions are going to be tested again. Will I be able to cope with the varying relationships that will be represented? Thinking about my family, I have only just realised that Harry's eight children, four of each gender, form a neat sandwich, a boy on each end and two in the middle, with two girls each side of them. Oh, how I love symmetry.

Mike and Faith have been warned about malaria and passed the message on. Another round of emails ensued, but it looks as though the consensus is that we will not be at risk, and anyway, the side effects of the medicine fill me with more horror than the disease. My pile of bits and pieces that should, may, or could be included in my luggage is growing, including a new camera, as the one we had with us last time has decided to become temperamental.

British Airways pilots have decided not to disrupt the Easter holiday plans of thousands of their countrymen – and women. That is one less thing for me to try not to think about.

Here in Finland it is snowing and a few degrees Celsius below zero, and Giles has let us know that we should prepare for March weather in the Lake District. I have no idea what that would be, but I think I need to prepare for coldish nights and warm days, so with an optimistic spirit, I'm going to pack some summery tops. I can't wait to get out of these winter clothes.

Chapter 12

Trip Two Commences

Pleasure and Pain

It's now the second week of April and I'm back at my computer screen attempting to digest and assimilate the last fortnight of the previous month. My heart is overflowing, and my thoughts run rampant as I contemplate the words I left unspoken, those uttered that should have been kept in check, the emotional outbursts at inappropriate times – and the fun. As I've lived in a foreign environment for some time, I loved experiencing the sheer abandon of English humour again. We played with words like a shuttlecock flying across the net. Mostly others initiated and played the field, but sometimes I managed to slice a whack myself. At other times, however, I missed my shots and fell flat on my face as my words were ignored or belittled.

The journey had started for me at about ten in the morning of a slightly frosty, middle-of-March day as Arto drove our car towards Tampere Airport. As we walked across the tarmac to have lunch at a service station nearby, I could hardly believe that only fifteen months earlier, I had been making this same journey with our three children, none of us knowing what to expect and whether we would find what I was looking for. I now knew what was possible.

Sitting in the tiny airport lounge waiting for the first flight of seven, making an average of one flight every two days for the next two weeks, I felt very alone. I had kissed Arto goodbye only an hour before, and the children several hours prior to that, and here I was contemplating time on my own – no one to leave my hand luggage with if I wanted the loo, no one to worry about – and no one to share my thoughts with.

Having found the correct set of seats to wait in at Helsinki Airport, I realised that this next flight would not be full of Chinese like before, as I heard French, German, Italian, Russian and various east European languages spoken around me. I found my window accommodation and wondered if I had a companion for the following nine hours. A bearded, greying man lowered his body into the adjoining seat and said hello. 'What accent is that?' I wondered. We exchanged a few pleasantries, including being offered a Finnish liqueur chocolate, which I declined, and discovered that he was Hungarian – a businessman judging by the papers he began to work on once take-off had been accomplished. I was grateful that he was not a talker and left me to explore the personal entertainment system we each had on the back of the seat in front of us, and to eat my meals in peace. He became engrossed in the chess games he was able to play on his system, and I wondered if he was actually playing against another passenger who was also linked up. I found a movie within the vast selection available that Tamara had recently been to see with her father and decided to watch it so that I could talk to her about it on my return.

The paperwork we had to fill in before disembarking had been condensed to one piece instead of three, which was less confusing. I had told Yoshi not to come too early to meet me at the airport as last time we had taken two hours to get through passport control and luggage retrieval. This time we seemed to be the only plane unloading, and as there were no little pieces of paper with useless information written on them to hand in before my little red book was examined, I sailed through the photo-inspection and case-removing and walked through to the receiving area half an hour after touchdown. No Sri Lankan face emerged from the crowd of Chinese ones, so my wait commenced. I like people-watching, trying to imagine how groups are related to each other, and seeing reunions with their hugs and smiles. I was treated to a show as, one by one, western males emerged and were greeted by oriental smiles and whoops of delight. I thought I had read that public signs of affection were frowned upon in this nation, but behaviour codes seemed to be changing, as couples kissed openly and fervently. My blood was more than likely running green at those moments.

After about forty-five minutes of this, I saw my daughter-in-law's face searching the space that stood between us. Now it was my turn to give and receive a hug. We took the maglev train and a taxi back to their flat, and I tried to tell my body that it was now midday and not early morning.

Since our last visit, Giles and Yoshi had moved to a neighbouring flat on the same floor and now had views in two directions. The rooms were bigger and contained new Chinese furniture that they had bought – wooden cupboards of various shapes and a lovely bench with a backrest, which served as an unofficial resting ground for various books and papers. The new L-shaped sofa was western looking and was where Yoshi showed me, on her laptop, their photos of Tibet from the previous summer. It was strange seeing these, knowing that riots were taking place there as I perused them, and that such a trip would be impossible less than a year later.

The sun was shining, and we went for a stroll and for lunch in my favourite little sushi bar. I was thrilled that it was still there. We bought some basic supplies like tea, coffee, and creamer for our upcoming trip as I didn't want my family to feel too homesick. The only thing that the children back in Finland had asked for was dried seaweed, so I bought a shredded variety for soups and some larger sheets that they like to roll around rice.

Giles came home from school late afternoon, looking smart in his suit and tie, and I flung myself into his arms. I didn't want to let go, but there were things to do. We went in a taxi to one shopping area where we needed to buy some tapes and a battery for various pieces of equipment that were going to be used during the trip. Ben was bringing a video camera to film our adventure, and had had no time to buy the materials he needed. On the journey, Giles tried to point out the world's tallest building, the Shanghai World Financial Centre, near the Jin Mao Tower and over 100 metres taller. I realised that it must be the building on which I had seen the worker ants on our first visit. A heavy mist prevented us seeing either of them.

After haggling for the electronic accessories, we emerged into a square and noticed a clear full moon. The metro beckoned and was followed by a walk, until we arrived at a Yunnan restaurant, where the waiters were dressed in traditional costumes. Delicious food arrived at our table, and I soaked up the atmosphere – dim lights, music, laughter, and conversation, very unlike my normal life. For just a while, I forgot that I lived in a small town with a husband who didn't seem to need change to his day-to-day routine. A trip to the restrooms was also different. Where there would normally be a mirror above the washbasin there was an open space through which I could see the washbasins of the other restroom, and if there had been a man washing his hands at the same time as me, I imagine we would have smiled, or even laughed, at each other.

By the time we returned to the twentieth-storey flat, I was exhausted, but sleep eluded me. I dozed on and off; during the latter, my thoughts spun out of control as they always do when in close proximity to my sons. I heard Giles getting ready and leave for school. I emerged and made myself a cup of coffee; Yoshi joined me soon after and then the cleaner who came twice a week. I found it peculiar to be sitting on the sofa talking to Yoshi while a stranger swept and mopped, filled and emptied the

washing machine, and did some ironing. After lunch, Yoshi final-
ised her packing and left for the airport, on her way to help her
grandparents celebrate their sixtieth wedding anniversary and
to see friends, family – and the sun. I was glad that I would be
seeing her again before my final departure from these shores.

Giles rushed in and out from school and to the airport,
leaving me with the computer. I found the kids cyber-connected
at home in Finland and 'spoke' with them on an instant mes-
saging service, trying to familiarise myself with a fruity laptop,
which felt like learning to swim all over again. It didn't help
that while I was trying to continue two written conversations at
home, one upstairs with Tamara and the second downstairs with
Thomas, Giles's friends in Shanghai, whom I had met in 2006 at
Yoshi's dance show, also started a typed dialogue, thinking that
I was Giles. Meanwhile, Thomas was attempting to send me a
document that I wanted and had forgotten to bring with me, so
I needed to keep checking my email page to see whether one, it
had arrived and two, I could open the attachment. I'm still not
sure that I wrote the right message to the correct person. Maybe
I told Giles's friend that I was missing him or her – I'm not even
sure which half of the couple I was talking to – or if I told them
that I couldn't open it, could they please try again.

I heard the code being entered on the door, the locks clicking
and whirring, and there they were – my two sons – the three of
us in one space, alone, the first time for twenty years. I had been
waiting for this moment, but no trumpets played, nor did fire-
works explode on the scene. Only in my heart. I rushed to Ben
and gave him a hug, trying to extract every ounce of pent-up
emotion.

Soon both of them were on their computers and checking
equipment. I was relieved when Giles suggested we go to the
local sushi bar for dinner, as that would only be a walk in some
kind of air – fresh or otherwise – as opposed to a taxi and metro
ride, and we had an early start in the morning. On our return,

Giles fired up the Wii system, the first one I had ever seen, and we played virtual tennis and boxing. It was quite unnerving to punch the air and see my opponent spin and dodge – not the kind of activity that I had been expecting.

I was the first to go to bed – exhausted and confused and unneeded. What had I been expecting? To hear words of consolation and understanding in the sushi bar? To be able to enter their world of intellect and sparring dialogue? At bedtime, to tuck them in and sing a lullaby? Those days had gone and would never return – except in my dreams.

Chapter 13

Lijiang Link-up

Reunions and Arrangements

Several faces hung over the barricade looking down on us as we ascended the escalator, one of them looking twenty years older than she was and as though she had been crying for hours, and I wondered what had happened. What had gone wrong this early in to our trip? As it turned out, Beijing pollution and food were what happened, causing swollen and puffy eyes, which subsided after a few days much to our relief, especially Jane's who must have wondered if she was destined to spend her whole holiday in the grips of an allergy.

The day before, three couples had arrived in Beijing, and I had been pleased to receive a text message in Shanghai from Mike: 'Have all arrived at hotel including Alfred. Are now going to have sleep for a couple of hours.' Alfred had already been in the city for several days, having travelled from Melbourne to Sydney, where his flight had been delayed by six hours, and then on to Beijing. His Chinese wife, also called Ruth, had asked her brother to meet him and sort out his mobile phone. We had received his new Chinese number before any of us had left our homes. Having experienced a small taste of the Chinese capital, they all left early the next morning for an internal flight to Lijiang where Ben, Giles, and I arrived shortly after them.

In Shanghai the airport had been crowded and noisy as my sons and I had found the correct check-in desk, and I wished I could have taken some photos of the Chinglish displayed on the instruction boards, but I didn't want to take the risk of a guard confiscating my camera. I contemplated storing some sentences in my memory, but thought they would take flight soon after they got there, and decided not to attempt such an I-must-have-dementia future moment. Security was thick with lines of bodies, some shuffling forward faster than others, or was it that we were going backwards? Giles and I got through in due time, but Ben's equipment caused a search. Finally the security personnel decided that he wasn't a reporter or photographer on his way to Tibet.

Following the introductions and gasps and hugs, the ten of us emerged from Lijiang airport, after some young women officials checked that the numbers on the tags on our luggage corresponded with the ones stuck on the back of our tickets, and we headed towards the taxi rank. There was no time to work out any logical groups of people to fill the vehicles, or even that the luggage belonging to the bodies in any one taxi went in the boot of the same car. Naturally, we weren't the only people trying to catch a lift, and so our chosen taxis were not neatly parked one behind the other. They did, however, all manage to arrive in the same place in the old town of Lijiang so that once again we were one group with mounds of luggage. A bike-truck appeared, and we loaded some cases into the back, and Giles walked with the peddler while the rest of us followed, some of us clattering over the cobbled paths with our wheeled-cases. The streams were flowing, and the willow trees bent over them were now in leaf, the bright green of the foliage declaring that spring was in progress.

Giles had chosen the same hotel where we had stayed fifteen months previously, and I was surprised at how much they had expanded the area of rooms. Ben had already said that he would share a room with Alfred, having planned to glean as much information as he could from the elder statesman, so that meant I would be with Giles, and we would need five double rooms all told. This was a pre-booking, and we had presumed that all the rooms would be the same. On our arrival, there was a different double situation as a girl I recognised from last time told us that there were only four of the basic rooms available, but we could have one suite at a reduced rate. Giles went to see it and came back with a huge grin on his face. The set of rooms was on the first floor, and we all decided that John and Ann, as the eldest couple present, should have it. I was busy making sure that everyone else found their rooms, so I was the last to go and see this reversal of fortunes. No one told me what to expect, but urged me to go and see. I walked in the door and was greeted by a large lounge, complete with a computer on a dark polished desk, two sofas, a flat-screen TV on the wall, a large shelf unit displaying various ornaments, and a bottle of alcohol ensconced in a holder on the coffee table. The bedroom door was immediately on my right, and as my foot stepped over the threshold, I started laughing and couldn't stop. It felt good to let go and relax, and feel the tensions leaving my body, almost as if they were dripping from my fingertips.

The bathroom spread along the far wall, and the only reason I knew the room's function was because the dividing wall was made of glass – clear and reflecting and revealing. The shower was on the left, the washbasin and mirror on the right, and bang in the middle, the toilet. From that moment on, we had our own Queen Ann, and I must admit that whenever she disappeared, I couldn't help but picture her on her throne. I discovered that there was a blind that could be lowered, although I didn't try to see if it landed on the floor at its longest, so it is possible that knees might still have been visible, but I never asked.

After we had all settled into our rooms, we went to the Wishing Well, my favourite café from our previous visit, where we all got to know each other as a never-before-assembled group. We met a young Chinese man there who spoke immaculate English and was visiting from Beijing. He took our orders and was ready to join in our laughter, which must have been echoing through the building. Following our pizza – yes, I did say pizza, but we got more adventurous as the days wore on – we separated into two groups. The three couples went to explore the town and climbed to a temple at the top of a hill. Jane, dressed up as a local horseman in a white fur waistcoat and brown hat (also made from an animal's skin) and brandishing a gun in the air, had her photo taken. Meanwhile Ben, Giles, and I walked to the travel company where we had hired our transport for Lanping last time, hoping to do the same. The place had changed management, and the inside of the office had been restyled, but Giles was able to make himself understood, and we waited while phone calls were made. A party came in during our wait, their guide tall, dark-skinned, and rugged. They sat on low stools talking and drinking tea.

Our vehicle-locater was short, but his smile was wide and stretched across his face like the sun. He found us a sixteen-seater van plus driver, who, on enquiry, would not need feeding or bedding during our three-day trip. He was to become one lucky fellow.

In the evening we all congregated in the royal lounge and agreed that having our own private space was a real bonus. There was plenty of room for the ten of us, and if we brought our own mugs, and some of us our small kettles, there was enough coffee, tea, and hot chocolate to have a drink together. The boys and I shared the details about our transport with the others, and asked Alfred to phone Mr Li to confirm that we would be arriving the day after next. We all sat transfixed as strange sounds issued from his mouth, ones that seemed to be understood at the other end of the line. The most pressing question was what present to take. None of us doubted that money would be useful, but such a commodity can easily be seen as too much – or too little. Giles came up with the suggestion of a computer for the grandsons who had been living there.

For breakfast next morning, we went back to the Wishing Well, but stayed downstairs this time. Jane asked the young man who had served us the day before to make a red flag with 'Our Boss' written in Chinese characters and English letters on it, to be presented to Giles. He didn't use it all the time, but sometimes he would produce it from his pocket and wave it above his head, as we had seen many Chinese tour group leaders doing. The locals thought it was very funny.

After breakfast we went on a walkabout to the new part of town. Before long, we were in an indoor market, and hopeful stallholders watched us and tried to interest us in their wares. The weather was much colder than we had been expecting; hence, most of our party decided to buy some long johns. I remember wondering where such a name had originated, and what John thought of it, but I never managed to ask him. I refused to buy any; I had spent the last six months wearing thick tights and socks, and had only just discarded them for spring. Granted, I was feeling chilly, but cold is relative. Two young girls were manning the stall where the others chose to make their purchases, and they were eager to sell as many pairs as they could. Their merchandise was piled high on trestle tables at the side of a staircase, and we all jumped with surprise when one of them, without warning, flung herself on top of a mound and disappeared beneath it to their storage space.

Emerging into the cool sunlight, we wandered past more shops, crossed the main street, and meandered along a new thoroughfare, which had a man-made stream running down the centre, and was lined with shops, most of which had been there on our last visit. Building was ongoing and had spread further towards the hills, blocking the views and encapsulating the whole country. 'Is this expansion, progress?' I wondered.

Realising that the shops we were now passing were either empty or still under construction, we turned into a side street and found a large square where the Lijiang International Ethnic Cultural Exchange Centre was situated at the top of a flight of steps. There was a dance and song show that evening based on love, fire, and air – or something equally ethereal and romantic – advertised as the *Mountains Rivers Show*. The advert promised a *Beautiful Night* and a *Mysterious World*. I remembered that a similar performance had been offered during our last visit. I didn't manage to get to it then, although I would have liked to have seen it, and this time proved a no-go as well.

I love living where I do, with the tranquillity and peace, the trees, and the lake, sometimes with a rainbow arched across it, at the bottom of the garden, but it would be liberating to spread my wings more often than, as a non-driver, I am able to. I couldn't fly in Lijiang by attending the show, but there were still more places to visit and surprises waiting in the wings.

Chairman Mao was also part of this square and towered over the place with his hand in salute. It seems that he is still revered as a mastermind in some quarters.

Our goal was to find a computer, and most of us left that choice up to Ben and Giles. We looked at new ones, but soon after found a shop, open to the street and the air, which sold reconditioned, second-hand ones. I'm not sure how long the rest of us stood on the pavement watching the world go by while they found suitable equipment, but it felt like the whole morning. We became the focus of every passer-by, and I loved smiling at them and seeing their responses, especially the children with their shy, head-to-the-side glances. When the transaction was complete, we had a monitor, keyboard, mouse, headphones, minicam, CPU with DVD-RW plus DVDs to carry. Ben and Giles did the honours, but before long, hailed a man with a bike-truck, and they and their loads sat precariously in the back and rode off into the traffic – not a sunset in sight. We met them back at the hotel, but not before taking some pictures near the two water wheels, which are the gateway to the old town and a symbol for Lijiang, at present my favourite place on earth.

Lunch or snack or coffee time – take your pick – was next. At home, my meal times are quite rigid as my stomach prefers it that way, but here there was no schedule, and I had to think what I wanted. It was after this meal that one of the older ones asked Giles and me if we realised that Alfred was talking about after Lanping. We had understood from Katharine and Christine that he wanted to spend the last days of his trip there, and not go to Chengdu with us, so Giles had bought him a plane ticket from Lijiang to Shanghai that would connect with his homeward flight to Australia. Cautiously I asked him where he would be staying in Lanping after we all left, and he stated, quite matter-of-factly, that he would be coming with us to Chengdu. This was a surprise to us all, but Giles and I decided we would try to accommodate him. We left the others and found a travel agent sitting in a kiosk in front of her computer, and she managed to get Alfred on the same flight as ours to Chengdu, and also on the flight that Ben, Giles, and I would be taking to Shanghai. His original flight from Lijiang to Shanghai was cancelled, but not refunded, and I suppose someone who had been told the flight was full got to make that journey.

The other thing that needed sorting out was an A4 black-and-white photo I had brought with me of Harry, taken in our living room, with Mum and all seven children, from Alfred at age thirty to Stephen aged six. This had always been a special photo for our family because Dad had died soon after it was taken. Alfred, who lived in London at that time, and Ivy, who had been living and working in France for several years, were not usually at home with us. As the photo was taken, none of us knew that there would never be another picture of its kind. My plan had been to give this copy to Mr Li as the last photo ever taken of Harry, and I had typed an explanatory sheet to go with it of who was who, dates of birth, and death (for Harry, Elsie, and Ivy), and which ones had visited him in March 2008. We all decided that it would be nice to frame the photo, which proved to be easier said than done. After the ticket purchases, Ben, Giles, and I set off in pursuit of a wooden surround. We tried several stalls that looked promising, but none had frames for sale. Using Giles's Chinese and sign language, we were pointed up a street that I hadn't been in before. We passed many small shops, all open to the elements, some spilling their goods onto the pavement, which was uneven and littered, but finally we found the one that we had been directed to. We started searching in the over-crowded space and found some wooden frames hanging on the back wall among charts and pictures. Having chosen the one that we thought the best size and style, we assumed the stallholder would appear, as if conjured up by a magician, from a neighbourly visit to an adjoining business, but no one had shown as much as an eyelash. Ben found some scissors lying on what looked like a desk and proceeded to make the photo fit the frame while Giles hung around the entrance hoping someone would come rushing up to secure a sale. Our previous experiences had all been too interfering. Mission accomplished, we waited with our present until a man rushed in. Giles didn't have much bargaining power over the price as it was already clear that we wanted his merchandise.

That evening, at my request, we went to the folk-singing restaurant for dinner. I was disappointed that no one was singing or playing as I had enjoyed the atmosphere so much last time. The place was empty apart from us clattering up the stairs to a chilly room where we re-arranged the tables. The food was good, and jokes filled the air as we talked about the upcoming trip – the purpose of this gathering.

Lijiang at night is captivating, with the light from red lanterns reflected in the streams. We wandered the cobbled streets, sometimes us girls arm in arm, peering at the array of goods for

sale, and at one point even jigging around, much to the amuse-
ment of the locals who might have thought that middle-age
westerners should show more decorum.

Chapter 14

Lanping Re-visited

Tears and Laughter

Most of us had brought all our luggage with us even though this tour was only for a couple of days. Last time, when we had gone to the Gorge, we had left unneeded things in storage and had found them in the same place, undisturbed, on our return. However, those who hadn't been with us on that first trip didn't want to trust the hotel with their extra. I only took my small backpack with a change of clothes, which was just as well as Giles had the computer to transport and had to give me his large haversack to carry full of food, water, and cooking equipment. The day before, I hadn't been able to believe how tiny the cooking ring was, as I had seen Giles folding it up into a space not much bigger than a matchbox. With back loaded and both hands full, I set off from the hotel grounds. Giles had ordered two bicycle-trucks the day before, as he knew it would be too early for anyone to be touting for trade. As we were waiting, I noticed the name of the guesthouse by which we were standing, and I asked John to take a photo of the four women. I asked Ann and Faith to stand under 'Ancient Town' and Jane and I stood beside them under 'Youth Hostel'.

When the bicycle-trucks arrived, the older of the two cabbies started flinging the computer and the others' cases into the open space behind his saddle. Wanting to do it carefully and neatly to maximise the space, Giles objected and tried to take over. The younger man spoke to his fellow countryman, which provoked the older one to answer back. Before long, words had turned into fisticuffs. We all looked on in horror – this was not the beginning we had envisioned. I can only think that the younger man's words had caused the older one to lose his dignity as the senior of the two, in a country where the respect and recognition of age are valued.

Tempers tamed and luggage loaded, we set off through the streets as some eatery stalls were setting up for business and facing a long day of cooking and serving. Giles's backpack proved almost too much for me as I lagged at the rear, taking the steps that brought the travel office into view at a slow pace. Even a tortoise could have ascended faster than I managed. The relief I felt as my donkey duties came to an end was immense. There we were, a crowd of foreigners, surrounded by luggage of all colours, sizes, and conditions, catching the attention of the few passers-by while waiting for a sixteen-seater bus to arrive.

The computer and luggage were stowed on and under the back seats, water and food stuffs arranged at the front, and the couples found double seats. Alfred sat behind the driver for communication purposes, and Ben, Giles, and I spread out along one side in the single seats. Less than an hour out of Lijiang, we stopped to stretch our legs and to marvel at the mountains that were visible in the distance, clouds hovering above and around them, unencumbered by man's intrusions. Between them and us lay agricultural land, some fields already showing green, others the deep red earth of this area, ploughed and furrowed – expectant. Seeing Ben standing with his video camera in this awakening atmosphere, I called his name and took a shot. As if by magic, my other son appeared, and I knew this might be my only opportunity, one I had been looking and hoping for – and needed. Before the bubble burst, I handed someone my camera and asked them to take a picture. Whether it turned out well or not, it would be framed and placed beside the one of the three of us on a beach, which had been taken more than twenty-five years before, when two little boys had been burying my legs under the sand, smiles on all our faces. Now they stood taller than me, and our smiles were more subdued. So much water had passed under that bridge shaped like a rainbow.

Several times during the journey, Ben jumped from the vehicle and ran ahead to find a good vantage point from which to shoot the van travelling along the road. We never knew if he would be up a tree or on the top of a hill. It took a while for the driver to realise that we didn't want him to slow down when he saw Ben in position. Like the rest of us, he had never been involved in the making of a documentary before, and it took us all some time to get used to having the long, cigar-shaped microphone thrust in front of our faces and being asked a question.

The road was curved and winding and rough in some places. Steve and Jane sat in front of the luggage leaving their seats at some spots and bouncing back to earth with a bang. They bore it all bravely and continued to smile. Spying a service station, we asked the driver to stop so that Giles could set up his kitchen. The day before, he, Ben, and I had bought ten packs of pot noodles of varying flavours, but his water container only heated enough for one at a time. Trying to be helpful, but not succeeding, I peeled the lids off some of the tubs and emptied the little packets found inside on top of the dried noodles sitting serenely in the bases. This would prove to be a mistake for some of our party, as they fanned their mouths and tried to take in fresh, non-burning air. During this process, Faith and Jane had gone to investigate the building that looked as though it might be the lavatory block. Indeed it was. The stench and missing tiles in the centre of the tiled floor in each cubicle – no doors, no wall, just a waist-high tiled partition – denoted the use for which this space was intended.

Although we had been told by the office manager that the driver would be seeing to his own stomach's needs, we offered him some of our food, but he declined. It wouldn't be long before he didn't. The area where we had been cooking and eating was strewn with litter, and it surprised me when some of our party added their empty, or otherwise, tubs to the general disorder of the place. Like a mother hen, I clucked around and retrieved what I could, and some like-minded soul took the bag I filled to a more appropriate place.

As we drove along, I tried to recapture my feelings from the last time I had made this journey, but it was impossible. Now I knew where we going, what was there when we arrived, and even more importantly the faces of some of the people we would meet. I could never go back to those emotions of uncertainty, adventure, and pioneering. The second time doesn't stir the adrenaline in the same way. Nevertheless, there was one burning question on my mind for most of the journey, singeing my peace. Where were we going to stay tonight and tomorrow? We had not booked a hotel, and from what I had found on the Internet, there weren't that many around, Lanping not having anything to attract tourists, apart from one species of monkey lurking in the forests in the vicinity. I had warned my family that the accommodation there would be quite basic, and, although I didn't elaborate as to how primitive that might be, I had my fears. In the past, I had had to live for many more than two nights in apologies-for-homes and knew I could cope with, if not enjoy, inferior-by-Western-standards sleeping arrangements. Some of the rest of my family, I had my doubts about.

The fields that had been barren last time were now springing to life with people, livestock, and greenery. Whole families could be seen working their land, either on their own or using a bullock to plough. Dark brown mounds of manure dotted the fields, waiting to be spread. Occasionally I saw colourful scarves adorning the women's heads, and sometimes the children would glance towards the road to catch a glimpse of the world going by.

As we entered Lanping itself and I saw the metal structure adorning one of the main roundabouts, it felt, in some special way, like coming home – something familiar, expected, and recognised. I seem to remember that we had decided to find a hotel first before contacting Mr Li by phone to arrange where to meet, but it might have been by accident that we saw a tall red building that looked as though it could be a hotel. How many stories there were, and how new it looked! This had not been advertised on the Web.

The next two days went by in a whirl, and I have had to ask my family to help me remember the order of events and who was doing what with whom at any given moment. The results were surprising and have made me wonder how many history books are accurate. To save myself from constantly typing *as far as I know*, I'll state now that what follows is the story of our time in Lanping according to Ruth.

We rolled up to the car park, a newly paved area in front of the hotel, and Giles and Alfred went to investigate. They seemed to have been gone for ages, but on their return had smiles on their faces. Was this going to be another surprise like the suite of rooms in Lijiang? Giles told us that there were rooms available, but not just yet, although there was one on the eighth floor where we could store our luggage until later. Alfred phoned to Mr Li, and before long a car rolled up, and two men at the young end of middle age emerged. They spoke with Alfred, and he introduced them to us as Mr Li's sons, but later we learned that one was his brother's son. Relationships cannot necessarily be translated from one culture to another, I've realised. In Finland, an uncle's wife does not become an aunt as she would in Britain, and I can remember the surprise I felt when my husband introduced one of his uncles as his aunt's husband. Maybe in China, all nephews are sons. Once the suitcases had been deposited in the empty room, we drove away from the hotel, following the car that now held Alfred in its frame, and proceeded to the older part of town. There we parked in a space that I did not recognise from the previous visit, which made me feel somewhat disorientated. Up a concrete slope and steps we traversed and entered the gateway that was now such a part of my life that sometimes I have seen it in my dreams. The court-yard was changed; it took only one glance for me to register that fact. The wall where I had said my farewells to Dad, and where Giles had gently registered my feelings, was now stacked high with wood. Red bricks were piled against the front of the house, and where the old rusty bath had stood beside the door, was a home-made wooden cart with bicycle wheels. One change I had been hoping for – the pear trees were in blossom, white as driven snow. The pile of rocks was now covered in plastic sheeting, and breezeblocks and wooden poles filled the rest of this lower space. The building materials continued up, adorning the platform to the left of Mr Li's room. There was an oblong wooden container half-full of hardening concrete next to a pile of sand; everything seemed to be in the process of changing, like much of this vast country – at least the parts that I had witnessed.

With ten of us plus driver added to the residents and various visitors, the place seemed to be crawling with people. It became apparent that Alfred couldn't catch everything of the Yunnan dialect that he had spoken as a child because since then, he had studied Mandarin Chinese. Consequently, we didn't get every-thing that was told to us – or asked. My first shock came when one of our party came up to me and said that Alfred had just said that they, meaning the members of my family who had lived here in the past, had never lived in the building that I had felt held my father's heart. Mine screamed and jumped and plum-meted. We had barely arrived at the destination that had taken so much planning, and now I'd been told I had been living a lie?

What had I done? Why had I thought that I could be the one to bring some of my family to their birthplace? I remonstrated and said that it had to have been built by Dad; just look at the English architecture, and don't forget the Morton box we had found. The next news was that yes, Dad built it – but for pigs and rabbits, the former enjoying the comforts of the downstairs amenities, the latter those of upstairs, no doubt benefiting from the rising heat from the swine. Never in my life had that word sounded more like a swear word than at that moment. Another member of my family suggested that satan was attacking me, but as I feel that he, she, or it is more often than not credited with what is human folly, I was not entirely convinced.

As with my previous feelings that Dad had returned here after the family's escape in 1944, as Mr Li had told us, I decided to try and keep my mouth shut and my feelings where they belonged, locked in my heart. I realised that sometimes it is not the '2 x 2 = 4' matters of life that are the most important, but the link between hearts. It was that building where I had connected with my father, and no one could take that away from me. It was also that structure which held the neatest surprise of the current trip.

Ben and Giles and some of the other men went to explore inside the house – by the following week, it might have been in a different state of repair. We were told that the people living in the neighbouring house owned half the land that the building was standing on, so the building work that we could see in progress was to divide the land in two. Before long, Dad's house would be history; we had made it just in time. The inside was more exposed than before, but the youngsters among us managed to climb, clamber, and hoist themselves up to the top floor where the famous Morton box resided. What they also discovered were wooden panels papered with copies of ancient newspapers, one of them dated 30 September 1938, the year that John had been born. There was an editorial about 'Holy

Laughter' and another page was entitled 'China's Millions' and
had the words, '— Hundred workers needed within two years.
An appeal from China to you.' The article underneath was entitled 'We Wrestle' and proclaimed itself as 'Being extracts from
the Short report of the China Inland Mission. Presented at [the
an]nual meetings held [in the] Central Hall, Westminster on
May 13, 1930.' The year of Alfred's birth. How had this paper,
as thin as it was, survived all these years, through wars, famines,
and Mao?

I no longer recall who first noticed the capitalised, large print,
boxed, and impressive advert in the centre of one page that had
us all laughing and oohing and aahing.

DO NOT MISS EASTER MONDAY'S
GREAT GATHERINGS
IN THE [ROY]AL ALBERT HALL

Although it didn't feel like it, today was Easter Monday. It
had taken us seventy years to heed the call.

The younger members of our party retrieved some of these
wall panels from the house and later borrowed a saw to cut
them into suitable lengths for putting into luggage. Some of
my family wanted a piece to take home, and Giles took the rest,
intending to use them in the future as wall decorations in his
dream home in Sri Lanka. Who got the 'Easter Monday' piece,
I don't know, but wherever it is, I know it will be treasured and
cared for. Mr Li's two grandsons became as interested as the
two of Harry's in obtaining some tangible objects to show from
this pilgrimage, so the Morton box joined the panels, along
with a pump contraption that looked as though it could have
been the one that Harry made for the paralysed serviceman, Lt.
Robert Wesselhoeft. There was no way of verifying what it had
been used for, but it gave me a warm feeling to speculate. On
re-reading the account on my return, I feel that the device we

found may well have been what Harry made for Wesselhoeft, as Kaplan arranged for a bigger version to be made for the time the sick man would be in the plane.

Someone also found a plastic doll's head, and Faith and I thought at first that it might have belonged to the one that Ivy was holding in the photo of her in the Morton box-turned-cart that had intrigued us. Ben had the presentation of 'Harry's Life' on his laptop, and we checked later just to make sure, but by that time, we had already been told – how stupid you both are – that plastic dolls would have been invented a lot later than the 1930s. Before discovering that I was not thinking straight, I had tried to clear decades of dirt from what had, I later hoped, been the pride and joy of a local Chinese girl. I also checked the old exercise books that had been retrieved from the dereliction, fingering their dirty, dusty pages as gingerly as I could, but they too were of later origins than we were interested in.

There was some excitement when Mr Li produced an old wooden box with FIRST AID and JUNGLE painted in bold white letters on the brown lid. Between the words was a red insignia surrounded by the words 'U.S. Army M[edical?] Department.' The M word was almost obliterated and to date, my endeavours to discover what the word was have proved fruitless, although my suggestion seems the most obvious. Mr Li had brought this box down from the area above his room, and when Mike asked me if I had seen up there, I replied no, not having realised that it was possible, or interesting. The old rickety staircase was covered in dust, and spider webs were the main occupants. The rooms above were in the same state, but contained several wooden boxes and trunks, which we were told had belonged to Harry. I wanted to pick up one of the smaller ones and put it in my luggage, but knew that was neither sensible nor necessary. Let them all rest in peace where he had left them over sixty years before. At age eighteen, I had used a large metal trunk with 'Fisher' stencilled on the lid, which had been to China and back, to take my belongings to college, but that is now lost to me, part of a world that I have no more to do with. Maybe part of me wanted to replace it.

Young women had placed bowls of fruit on the table near Mr Li's room and people were sitting on the sofas and milling around. Then two kindergarten-height tables were arranged with matching-sized stools on the raised concrete below his quarters, one table next to the trough for concrete. Bowls of hot food started arriving. And the beer bottles. It was strange for me to see my family, who used to be teetotallers like our parents, swigging down the golden nectar. I rarely sip anything stronger than passion fruit juice, childhood behaviour and restraints staying strong in my system, but my family, who have all retained the 'faith of their fathers,' are quite content to have changed their drinking habits, apart from Faith. This was only an observation on my part – no judgement intended.

The food was good and plentiful, although the lumps of pork fat with scraps of flesh hanging on for dear life rather turned my stomach, and I stuck with the more vegetable-looking concoctions. Our driver had been included in the meal – eating it, not being eaten – and this would continue during our time with these hospitable people.

As the meal ended, some of us made our way down to what had become a building site, and photos were taken beside the open doorway of the old house, firstly Mr Li with the three who had been born here, and then Steve and I joined them – five of Harry's offspring standing on Chinese soil that he had trodden and tilled.

By this time, another son and daughter of Mr Li had arrived, and it was group-picture time. Giles, as Tamara wasn't present, had been playing with the little dog, and it got over-excited. We arranged ourselves in two rows, standing and sitting, Giles in the middle of the front row on a low stool, when, without warning, the dog crept up behind him, pushed his snout underneath his sweater and began licking his back. It was impossible for Giles, or any of the rest of us who could see what was happening, to keep a straight face.

After the pictures were taken, we divided. Now the fun started, if that is what you call small groups of people not knowing what the other small groups are doing or even how many small groups there are. This was probably the time when language barriers were at their highest – sky-high, looking back. I still do not know how we were split up, but there seemed to be a feeling that the hosts were heading us towards the gate and the van. Once there, Alfred, John, and I were shepherded along by the son who had come to the hotel on our arrival, and taken on a tour. We walked along what was a main street for this part of town, drawing stares as we proceeded, having no idea where we were going or where the others were. It was rather unnerving. We walked fairly slowly, at Alfred's pace, until we were ushered into an alley and through a metal gateway into a courtyard. Modern buildings were on two sides, and the son showed us his room and garden, vegetables already green and growing. It would be more than two months before I would even be able to sow seeds at home.

We took some photos, sat on some low stools outside his home, were ushered out, and walked back to the car park. We immediately got in the van and found ourselves driven to the same spot where we had just walked from and found the others there waiting. It had all been most confusing.

I have since found out that while we were on a walk- and sit-about, the following was happening. All the messages were addressed to me.

Giles's words: 'Ben and I were in the roof of the house; we were then led on foot to where they thought you were, but you had already left to come back, so we stayed there until you came back.'

Mike's words: 'I personally don't recall you, Alfred, and John

being taken to the son's house, although I do remember waiting
for some of the family as we were not sure where they were. In
the meantime, we wandered around the premises, walked up
and down to the bus a few times and 'talked' to neighbours in
the house next to your dad's. I also spent quite a bit of time
exploring and taking photos in and around your dad's house.'

Jane's words: 'We were wondering where you were and what
to do; we went several times to the minibus, but no one was
there, so eventually we went to the minibus and stayed there.'

Therefore – we were missed, even if not everyone was quite
sure who was missing.

The hotel lobby was immense, round, and shiny, and looked
as though a party of two hundred travellers could fit comfortably within its perimeters, and even use it as a skating rink. Giles
dished out the key cards and said afterwards that he hadn't
known he was giving us a corner room, which resulted in us
having views towards the far distant, snow-capped mountains
plus the city square in one direction and a different range of
peaks, the school, and surrounding town in the other. We all
retrieved our luggage from the room on the eighth floor and
took the lift to the twelfth.

The beds were huge, and the floor carpeted, which I don't
have, as Finns need to be able to take their floor coverings outside and bash them every week. This means rugs are all the rage.
The curtains were floor-length and lined with dark-inducing
material. The bathroom was stocked and even included an
emery board, which left a blue shadow across your nails. The
kettle worked, and paper cups were supplied. The cups were
rather a letdown – such comfort should have had chinaware.
This was the accommodation that had concerned me the most,
but it turned out to be the best we used for the whole time we
were a group of ten.

Needing to give some consideration to all that had been said that day about pigs and rabbits, I decided to have a soak in the bath, as opposed to the sauna that is my usual preference these days, while the others went to check out the local night-life. They had the more successful mission. I turned on the tap, and with one hand checked the temperature of the water and with the other held the plug, ready to put it in the hole as soon as the water was warm enough. Having lived through a drought in the middle of the Welsh countryside where we relied on well water, wasting water is one of the things that I get angry about, even if it is only a tensing of the stomach muscles. Cold water continued to run into Lanping's drainage system, and I wished I could save it for my indoor plants at home. Such crazy thoughts to be going through my head. At some point, I couldn't take it any longer and turned off the tap.

When the others returned, they were full of stories of the communal dancing in the square, all different ages moving to the piped music, the pool tables out in the open, and the way in which Giles had been able to engage some youngsters by playing hand games with them without the need for a common language. Mike felt the young people had been well behaved, feelings prompted by comparing their behaviour to some nearer home maybe.

We had seen no other foreign faces since our arrival, and, as we were a party of ten – except when some of us decided to try to have a bath – we attracted attention as we moved around. It wasn't only the locals who had noticed us. On the second day, one of the young men who had served us at reception came up to our floor and apologised profusely as he handed us ten forms that the police wanted filling in. The hotel had already viewed our passports stamped with visas and had, we imagined, photocopied them for their records. Why weren't the authorities satisfied with that? I did wonder whether they were more paranoid than usual because of the riots that were ongoing in

Tibet *and* the fact that Ben was carrying a video camera with a long microphone around with him.

The following morning, Alfred and John disappeared with the nephew to find the place where their mother had been buried. We had all thought that it was far outside the town as the older ones had been told that as she was a foreigner and a woman, Harry had not been allowed to bury her closer to home. That family myth would soon be shattered. The day before, when this expedition was being arranged, John had asked, with tears in his eyes, whether Ben and Giles would go with them. He must have felt he would be safer with younger company. Looking at the photos now, I've found that the two Chinese grandsons were also there, and the symmetry gives me great pleasure.

While they were gone, the three ladies came to my room, and we had a roller-coaster morning of emotions. I had awoken and got up before Giles, trying to fulfil my morning rituals of bathroom and dressing as quietly as possible. The sun had been shining behind the thick curtains, and I had stood there, feeling the warmth of the rays touching my outer and inner selves. A group of early risers had been doing their exercises in the square, and the mountains looked magnificent in the distance, a feast for eyes that lived in flatness.

Each morning since we had left Shanghai felt a little like walking on eggshells. I was grateful that my son didn't mind sharing a room with me, but it was an unusual situation for both of us. I suppose I had been thinking that we would go down to breakfast together after he was ready, but before I realised what was happening, he had put his coat on and was out of the door. I could not face leaving the room, going down in the lift, and finding the restaurant on my own. I stayed where I was, staring at the door, the old insecurities raising their heads like dragons from the deep, their open mouths spewing fire into my thoughts.

Busy yourself; do something. Anything but standing here, let-ting the past interfere with the present. That has all gone.

I have not stayed in many hotels, life not presenting me with those possibilities, and those I have were at the cheap end of the scale. Nevertheless, I did know that maids came and made the beds and tidied the towels and generally did what I would do for my personal things. They must love me or think I'm crazy. I always make my own bed, thank you very much, and I can put my own towel neatly on the rail and place any rubbish I make from toothpaste or soap in the bin myself. So ... I made my bed, placing the golden silk throw at the end of it and started to do Giles's as well. That is when the tears started flowing and would not stop. Such a simple action, but filled with such ter-rible pain – for all the times I had been unable to do that for him and Ben.

When I heard the tentative knock at the door, I approached it and peered through the spyhole. Faith, who had helped me through many dark moments, was on the other side. 'Are you all right?' It's quite sad that she needs to ask that question when-ever we meet. I tried to keep my emotions in check, but couldn't find the strength. She knows me too well to play games.

'Why did I have to leave them?' – the question that is never far from the surface, and in the physical proximity of my two older sons, was like a boil waiting to burst through skin as fragile as a butterfly wing. Even three years of writing didn't take the sting out of the scorpion's tail, and at the end of that process, I came to the realisation that there was nothing that could, unless I stop loving my children as their mother.

Ann and Jane joined us, and they provided the excuse I needed to pull myself together, and we sat on the chairs and the bed and shared stories and jokes, some more risqué than I had thought my family were capable of producing, and enjoyed each other's company. The only time I can participate in such gatherings is with my students, and they are mixed groups, not

a conducive atmosphere for unburdening and sharing one's
inner life, and anyway, they want to practise using English, not
be used as shrinks. I have since discovered that while we were
having a women's circle, Steve had a quiet morning in his room,
and Mike, after reading, went exploring near the hotel.

The men returned, and we learned that Victoria had been
buried in what is now a ploughed field, behind Mr Li's building.
So close, but we had had no idea. His parents were also buried
there, and while Ben and Giles had been showing him and his
family the slide show of 'Harry's Life', he had recognised his
parents in one of the group photos that I had chosen to include
in the presentation. We can only assume that they had been
some of Harry's congregation. John had had the most moving
experience, hearing Mr Li play some old choruses on his mouth
organ and being able to sing along with him, in Chinese. The
grandsons had also captured his heart. In his words, 'The grandsons picked me some pale mauve blossom, which I wanted to
treasure. In those two short days, we came to love those boys
as if they were our own grandsons.' I can only imagine what he
felt, connecting with the mother who died when he was three-
and-a-half years old.

The nephew and Mr Li wanted to take us all to lunch. We
followed them out of the hotel, and before long I realised that
we were on the same street where we had eaten on our first
trip, only now the place was shuttered, and we were being led
to another eating-place on the opposite side of the road. Up a
flight of stairs, along a narrow corridor with various sized rooms
on the left and windows on the right, we found a young girl
hastily dusting and wiping down some tables. Stools were produced to accommodate our group of thirteen. Yes, the driver
was still with us, enjoying the same food as us and – a room in
the hotel, the one on the eighth floor that had been storage for
our luggage. We speculated that he would have never seen such
a place before. He did not appear to have any bags with him,

and we imagined that he would have slept in his means of livelihood without our generosity.

The food was good, and we learned, by observing, that we
could put any rubbish, including bones, on the floor. I remembered our Plan family, and shuddered to think what they thought
of us putting our shells on the food table. Following lunch, we
ventured out to explore the town, garnering stares wherever
we went, especially as we decided to check out the local indoor
food market, the ground swarming with discarded leaves and
debris, and in some places running like a streamlet. The goods
on sale looked fresh, and many of the vegetables I could give
no name to. As I love them in my diet, I would have liked to
try some, but this was not the occasion. Passing through the
food area, we came to the clothes and hardware, some tables
covered in tiny items, many of which looked the worse for wear,
although they may well have been new. Few vendors were in the
process of haggling or clinching a deal, and life seemed rather
static and airless. Back on the street, we passed a man sitting on
the pavement with a budgie in a budgie-sized cage. It could just
turn around and seemed to be doing so in a frenzy. We think
he was some kind of fortune-teller, but how the bird helped,
we had no idea. On the opposite side of the road were modern
spaces filled with electronic equipment. Two worlds living side
by side. Jane bought some loose tea from a small supermarket
after checking with Alfred that she had the right name for the
flavour she had enjoyed at Mr Li's house. She and Steve were
planning to have a China event at their church after their return,
and she was already preparing. I was searching for local handicrafts, but there were none to be seen, another sign that this was
not a tourist destination.

Whenever I had made searches for Lanping, there had been
hundreds of sites about the zinc mining in the area, and I assumed
having now seen the huge hotel we were staying in, that it was
intended for businessmen planning to invest in China's wealth.

One morning we heard explosions on the humbling mountains and could only imagine what the coming years would do to the serenity of this place, not to mention the pollution, as chemicals invade the atmosphere of this town nestled in a valley.

❧

The time had arrived for us all to go to the burial site, but especially so that Faith could visit. As we walked there, I had no inkling how this was going to affect me. Some donkeys laden down with red bricks in baskets slung on each side of their bodies passed us on the sloping path to the residence, and we found a group of people emptying them out as we made the top of the hill. We followed the locals behind the house. It was not an easy walk: stony, uphill, and slippery in places. No one knew what to say once we were there, all lost in their own thoughts and memories – or lack of them – and inner stirrings. I have known for a long time, as long as I can remember knowing, that I am only here, living life, because Faith's mother died at her birth. It has been a sobering thought and one I cannot deal with sometimes. Standing on that ground, looking down on the red soil covering the area that held their mother and sister, my heart leapt and screamed. For the first time I felt that both mothers were mothers to all of us. There was no difference; each of them had given each of us, life.

We congregated together, and Mr Li again played a tune on his harmonica. I recognised it straight away and was singing in my heart along with the melody. 'In the sweet bye an' bye, we shall meet on that beautiful shore.' It surprised me that the others couldn't place it, but their souls must be full of more modern fare, whereas I am stuck in a time warp. I did not attend the funerals of either of my parents, and this simple ceremony, no words spoken because there was nothing to say and no common language with which to say it, was my funeral for both of them, as well as for Victoria. Faith's words summed it up as the enchantment was broken and we started to move off.

'That was the nicest funeral I have ever attended.'

We made our way back through the fields being prepared for sowing and followed our leader to the derelict set of buildings that we had been shown before. Alfred became more animated here, pointing out the room where Dad had developed his photos, where they had slept and where a dozen other daily activities had taken place. From listening to the translations that were going around and Alfred's comments, it became apparent that Dad continued using these rented buildings for most of the duration of their stay. The present owner of the property dropped by, whether asked or merely curious about the crowd of foreigners on his land, and I would have loved for somebody to try to find out if he was a direct descendant of the man in the presentation who is labelled, 'Our landlord'. If he was, he could have had some records from that time, but I didn't want to get in the way of Alfred's reminiscences, so I held my tongue.

More group pictures were taken in that setting, and then we were taken through a lightless space that Alfred said had been Harry's darkroom. At the back was a large vegetable garden, the rich soil ready for planting, some greenery already in evidence. I am still not sure if Harry was allowed to use it for the same purpose, but maybe he was. My few memories of the years we shared are of him in the garden, tending, among other things, his tomatoes, runner beans, and marrows.

Now we had to return to the hotel and say our goodbyes. As we descended the path from the old Fisher home and came close to the car park, we saw a group of children playing together. Giles tried to entertain them, but it was only when we were below them and about to enter the van, that their faces turned to smiles. As we entered the vast foyer of the hotel, a group of young people dressed in national costume emerged from a meeting room opposite the entrance. The timing was perfect as it looked as though they had been asked to exit as we entered. Maybe they had. An older man in a western suit and tie started flapping his arms about, and I think we all felt that we should get out of the way, but he was trying to get us to stand still. His charges lined up in a row; his arms were being used as a baton, and they commenced their song. It ended after a few minutes, and during our clapping, he walked along our row, shook our hands and saluted each of us in turn. This was not a military situation and did nothing to put us at our ease or feel welcomed, if indeed that was his intention. Bizarre behaviour. It was noticeable that he did not offer his hand to any of our Chinese friends, whether out of rudeness, because of politics, or different stations in society, we will never know. The young-sters trooped out of the door, and I stopped one of the young men and asked someone to take my photo with him. We made our farewells, and I'm sure that most of us knew that we would never see Mr Li again.

〜

You may be wondering what happened to the computer, and I have left it to last because it caused two of my getting-into-a-flap moments. Soon after our arrival, while Giles was still in the hotel and Mr Li's son and nephew had made their appearance in an 'oh, look what a good car he's got,' from those who know about such things, Alfred could not contain his excitement and told them that we had brought a computer for them. There had been a feeling, definitely on my part, that this would be a surprise gesture for Mr Li's benefit, and would be for his grand-sons. Of course the rest of us were hearing nothing in English, but when the men started looking as though they wanted to see the computer and Alfred said that they could take it in the car with them, now, I panicked, seeing the computer disappearing into the sunset in a cloud of dust never to be seen or heard from again. We had all contributed to this present, and I wanted it presented in a careful and considerate way. Before my gasket blew, I saw Giles returning and dashed towards him, garbling my message that those men want to take the computer, and you can't let them, it's not for them, it's supposed to be a surprise, and who are they anyway? You would have thought a volcano had erupted somewhere. He told me to calm down, and I left the situation in his capable hands. The cat was out of the bag, but at least the computer was still in the bus, even if there would be no more surprises.

When we left the old house area later that afternoon and made our way down the slope towards the car park, there were more rumblings about the computer, and it was the older men who still wanted it put in their car. I remonstrated and felt panic rising in my chest. The grandsons were hovering, showing great respect for their elders, but they could not hide the excitement they were feeling. Confusion reigned because of language and intention barriers, and in the midst of it, I remembered that I had failed to give the photo in the non-haggled-for frame to Mr Li. I produced it from the minibus and gave it to the nephew, explaining the faces on the picture itself and my words on the explanatory sheet. Then inspiration hit. I asked Alfred to explain to the older men that Harry's grandsons, Ben and Giles, had wanted the computer for Mr Li's grandsons. More symmetry; still my speciality. That seemed to do the trick, and the boys and Giles took the equipment up the slope to the house, the whole process, as far as I know, being filmed by Ben. Stephen and Jane were still there and saw it arrive. Is it still there, or has it been transferred to some other house or business? Who knows? – but at least our wishes were made known, and we can only hope that this younger generation of Lanping inhabitants will have smiles on their faces when they remember our visits and think about the man and his wife who gave the best years of their lives to their hometown.

Chapter 15

The Gorge

Climbing and Confusion

The day started early: before dawn, it felt like, but it was already light, and there were a few people also commencing their days as we rambled through the cobbled streets of the old town towards the pick-up point. Giles had hired the same driver personally for a day trip to Tiger Leaping Gorge, one of the deepest in the world.

As we were preparing to leave, Mike appeared and said that Faith had been breathless in the night and had decided not to come. She had not shared much about being in Lanping, but I knew that it had affected her deeply, and two four-hour, bum-jumping journeys would not have helped her physically. I offered to stay with her, but Mike insisted that he would, which was a disappointment for me, as I didn't need to do this trip, wanting to preserve my memories from the last visit, and some quiet time with Faith would have been welcome.

On our last night in Lanping, after a trip to the square where John, Jane, Ben, and Giles all attempted to join in the line dancing, and a group of young girls, led by the most confident, brash ten-year-old I have ever met, practised their little English with us, we ventured upstairs in the hotel and found a space that felt like it didn't quite know what to do with itself, and had some snacks, Chinese fashion – popcorn, various nuts and seeds, soft drinks, and hot chocolate. We would be leaving the following morning and needed to decide what to do the day after, the last one before we left for Chengdu. Giles offered a few options, including the Gorge, and each person was asked his or her preference. I chose not to participate as I had already been there and didn't want my choice to sway the result.

'And our twelve points go to … The Gorge.'

Another several-hour journey lay ahead of us. We had left early because Giles wanted as much time as possible up the mountains, and thought we could get to the beginning of the road to the Gorge before the ticket office opened. It's possible that the driver knew this as he seemed to be taking his time, although we knew that he could drive faster on bendy roads. This office was a new initiative, started in 2004 when tourism began taking off, and it was merely a small room by the roadside on a public road with no barriers or entrance gates. Presumably it was some kind of local enterprise – money for nothing. The office was already manned and ready for a day's exploitation, and someone joined us in the van and did a headcount. Giles used some of the older faces to get a senior reduction, but the locals insisted on seeing some proof. Our senior citizens were chuffed by that. The taker of tolls perused what was offered and seemed satisfied, but I doubt that she understood what she was looking at. Discounts were offered and accepted.

We passed the modern complex of buildings that had been at a rudimentary stage during our last trip; they looked as though they had been transported from the Land of Oz, but we continued along the dirt, not yellow-brick, road. At a bridge, the driver started to turn right. Giles's reaction was quicker than mine, although I also knew that last time, we had gone straight on. We still don't know where he was trying to take us, or why. Reluctantly he changed course, drove on, and pulled into a car parking area situated before the tunnel in the rock face. He refused to go any further, even though the day before, Giles had shown him clearly on a map where we wanted to go. Thinking about it later, we imagined that as a non-local, he would have been treading on the toes of those who saw the area as their patch – the local Mafia. The wind was blowing and not coming from a warm direction. Collars up and scarves round necks, we had to find some further transport. A truck with one seat by the driver, three behind, and space for livestock at the back released its travellers and beckoned to us. The ride on a seat was bad enough as we travelled over pot holes on the rocky road, so I have no idea how Steve, Jane, Ben, and Giles arrived in only four pieces after standing in the open space behind us.

On arrival at Tina's Guesthouse, where we had stayed pre-viously, we ordered some breakfast, and I looked out at the mountains and could not believe that I was back here again. I saw myself sitting in the sun on the last day of a man-made year, sharing my thoughts with a notepad. There was no sun today, and the March breezes felt colder than what we had experienced in December.

Alfred and I were not going to attempt the climb that Giles, Yoshi, and the three Finnish children had achieved, but John decided to accompany the boys and the youngest couple among us for the first, easier part, leaving us to wander along the road, not exactly flat but not difficult either. We met a young Australian couple along the way, and, as they were busy looking down on the water and admiring the mountains either side, I offered to take a picture of them together, shyness not able to keep me company in these surroundings. His camera was bigger, better, and more elaborate than mine, so I asked him to check what I had taken, and he requested 'less road' at the bottom. That slight adjustment turned the next picture from ordinary into an adventure. It reminded me of the photo that Giles had taken of Yoshi in a ballet pose, arms held above her head, facing the mountains in the background, looking as though she were standing on the edge of the world.

On our return, Ann was back, not having ventured far at all; we ate, read, and chatted to various travellers who passed through, including two Swedish boys who had linked up with a Dane. They spoke English well, with accents that were in some way familiar, and were surprised when I told them that I lived in a neighbouring country, but not surprised that my children find Swedish, which is the second official language in Finland, difficult to learn.

I longed to go outside to my spot and sit in the sunshine, but the weather didn't oblige, except for one short spell of cloud clearance. We hadn't seen John for some time and were just commenting on the fact when he appeared around a corner and asked us to come and meet some people he had met on the trail. He had climbed the hill for about one kilometre, met two Americans on their way down and decided to join them for the descent. Ann followed John, with Alfred and me at the rear, and we found them seated at an outside table waiting for some food to be served. One was older and the uncle of the younger, and they seemed to have an amiable relationship. I sat and listened, as I had no idea what John and they had been talking about, or what they had in common. Alfred shared some thoughts with them, and I hoped that none of us was holding them up or interfering with their plans. These got discussed at some point, and when it was ascertained that the rest of our party would be returning from their mountain trek at four o'clock, and that we had a minibus waiting, which would be taking us back to Lijiang, we discovered that was where they were heading. They were offered, or asked for, a lift with us, and as we had plenty of room – we were two party members short and had no luggage with us – it was agreed upon. This was arranged at about two o'clock, and they set off for some more exploration to fill the time – which went slowly, like watching a second hand work its way around a clock face in a dentist's waiting room. Every now and again, one of us, or some combination of us, went out and stared up into the grassy space which should contain four bodies, sooner rather than later, zigzagging their way down to join us.

Dead on the dot of four o'clock, I received a text message.

16.00 Giles to me 'Had a few issues – but have left half way house, will be back asap.'

Half Way House was the eatery that should have been accomplished a long time ago, so there was no need to continue looking for specks on the slopes. I had just passed that message on to the others, so that they too knew they were going nowhere anytime soon, and then my mind naturally began producing ideas about what the 'issues' might be – falling off slopes, attacks by yaks, food poisoning, dehydration – the possibilities were endless – when there was another beep.

16.07 Jane to me 'Hi ya have u seen the others?'

What? Was this one of the issues that Giles had nonchalantly referred to? Seven minutes ago, they, no, let's check again, no, he didn't mention *who* had left Half Way House, but *surely*, he would have said if anyone was *missing*? Discussion with the others ensued as I clutched my out-of-the-ark Nokia, which may not play music, take photos, or wash the dishes, but worked very well between mountain and valley, *and* between China and Europe – unlike some of those among us who weren't able to text at all.

Those deliberations took several minutes. I tried phoning. No answer. With my thumb, I pressed in several questions, all of which I dreaded the answers to.

16.12 Me to Jane 'What do u mean? Are u with s b and g? Where r u?'

Nothing. No reply. I tried phoning again.

No answer.

16.16 Me to Giles 'Thanks. Message from Jane came after yours. R u altogether now?'

No reply, but

16.18 Jane to me 'Ruth f has rang twice could ann ring her I not got her'

Ruth Fisher, my original name, but now belonging to two of my brothers' wives, had been keeping us informed of her and Paul's doings, as well as us letting them know where we were and what we had been doing. Paul was the only living sibling who had been unable to join us, and we all felt that loss during the trip. If Ruth had tried to phone, twice, and not just text, what was wrong with Paul? That could be the only reason she would phone.

Out came Ann's phone, each of us now with our thoughts up Slopes and back in S—, our hometown where John and Paul still reside. Ruth answered and had no idea why Jane should think she'd been calling her. One problem out of the way. So what had Jane meant? Suddenly it dawned on me that I had phoned her twice, and she must have only glanced at the incoming calls, saw 'Ruth', and her brain went skimming over land and sea instead of down the mountain.

That crisis solved, we could only wait. Jane hadn't mentioned being on her own again; no one was sending any more messages, and no one was answering their phones; what else could we do?

After what seemed like a whole day, we made out four tiny shapes descending the slope, and with the help of the zoom on my camera, we could tell that the colours matched our companions. They made some jokes about the text messages, because, of course, I had completely fallen for their teasing. Looking back, it was funny, but at the time, I could only cry with relief that they were all down safely. Giles knows I'm a bit of a worrier, well, a lot if I'm honest, but I found it hard to be teased in a situation where we had no idea what might have befallen them.

Jane had actually fallen and hurt her hand, but had struggled bravely on and had still been able to wind me up.

We hired two vans back to our bus, found the driver asleep or contemplating the mountains or admiring his new trainers, and there were some interesting conversations during the return journey with the Americans.

Faith was better, and we were all tired, especially Steve and Jane after their strenuous hike, which can't have been too easy for a couple of fifty-somethings. They had put me to shame anyway. Our meal that night included snails, which Giles ordered for a joke, I hope, as there were many left in the dish when we departed.

Chapter 16

Chengdu

Pandas and Parks

Our plane left Lijiang for Chengdu at 8.20, and we would need to leave the hotel at 6.15. This time it was dark, and there were no streetlights or illumination from the stalls. Neither were there any men and truck-bicycles, so we made quite a clatter as we traversed the rough-paved paths of my favourite place, for the last time.

The day before, on our return from the Gorge, Giles had asked the driver, who had received food, drink and luxurious surroundings in which to sleep for two days in Lanping, even though we had been told that the price did not include those perks, whether he would come for us early the next morning to take us to the airport. He gave his price, and Giles tried to haggle it down, as is expected. The guy wouldn't budge. Hearing this story later, I thought that he could have offered to do it for nothing. Giles said that if he had agreed, he would have given him double. It was his loss. He may have taken advantage of the situation, but it had been useful having four wheels plus driver on call whenever we needed to move around in Lanping.

The airport was fairly busy, and it was early. Too early for me to be reacting to people's comments, which I did, raising my voice too much and making a spectacle of myself. Apologies from me to them ensued, and the more sensible me told the other me to keep its thoughts to itself.

This was the only checkpoint of the whole journey where everyone had to take off their shoes, so the queue shrank about as quickly as a slug on a stroll through a cabbage patch. Ben's cameras took some scrutiny again, but the old wooden boards covered in ancient newspaper, some of which hadn't made it into suitcases, didn't cause a blink or raised eyebrow.

John made friends with a group of young women in the waiting room, proudly showing them his passport with Yunnan, China as his place of birth. Alfred and Faith were asked to join the gathering, and yet another group of people knew why we were in their country.

Chengdu airport was large, but we didn't have to hang around, as Giles had already made private arrangements with the young woman who had taken his phone booking at the hotel. She had offered to pick us up at the airport, take us to the hotel, book tickets and transport for a show in the evening, and arrange for vehicles to take us back to the airport for our flights out. As planned, she was waiting with a plaque with Giles's name in bold letters and led us through the car park to two waiting vans. They were not quite big enough for all of us plus luggage, but we squeezed in, some more squashed and uncomfortable than others. When we parked in what was almost a back alley, and she alighted, I realised that this was not part of the hotel service, more a quick buck on the side – enterprising and lucky, if you weren't caught. We drove around the corner and found ourselves in front of the hotel. It was not as pleasant as in Lijiang, older and with an unpleasant smell lingering in the rooms, but the sheets seemed clean, and it was not going to be a long stay.

The lobby had some racks of tourist literature, and I found some English ones to read. This is a sample from one of the leaflets. '*A clean crystal stream, flanked by trees on both sides, S.... River*

is a beatingpulse, stringingtogetherthecultures of water,bridge,
teaandpoem with Chengdu characteristics, embodying the person-
ality of Chengdu: "Being good like water, with water as artery,
and cherishing green beauty, withcultureasthesoul.'

That was so hard to type. I automatically made spaces at the
end of words, and at the moment, there are many red and green
squiggly lines in evidence on my computer screen. And honestly, the words did start stringing together at that point.

Nearby was a café where we had some lunch, followed by
a trip on an open-top bus to see the city. It felt warmer than
previous days, but the wind was rather strong on the top deck
from where we viewed the busy metropolis, one of the largest in
China with a population of around eleven million. If any young
people walking on the pavements caught our eye, they were
eager to wave at us; the older ones more wary. After about thirty
minutes, Giles headed towards the stairs, and we all followed
suit. Managing to cross the busy thoroughfare, we arrived at a
park with a large wooden entrance. Tickets bought and shown,
we entered an area full of greenery and blossoms. It was a stunning sight, especially for me, who now lives with snow and dark
for half a year at a time, and who was born in spring and finds its
late arrival each year a heartache.

This area was famous for some poet who had lived many years
ago, and if you're interested, you can check on the Internet. He
was well-known throughout China, and I seem to remember that
he had a thatched house. The ambience was calm and peaceful,
but the water in the various ponds was muddy and unappealing.
We found a different kind of watering-hole and joined many
families and groups of people sitting in the sun around tables,
enjoying each other's company and the relaxing atmosphere.
We ordered some herbal teas, some more refreshing looking
than others, and John made friends with a middle-aged man
who spoke good English. He was brought over to our tables,
and yet another bunch of Chinese heard our tale.

I had been hoping that at least once in the trip, I could dress up and wear my mid-heeled, open sandals. If I didn't do it now, I never would. My feet were cold, but I felt good. The vans met us at the door of the hotel, and we were whisked off through the city night. Surprisingly enough, both vehicles arrived at the theatre at the same time, although we had been weaving in and out of traffic all the way. Our private guide gave us each a small bottle of water and led us upstairs to our seats, in the back row.

My ticket gave me the following information: *Sichuan opera 'Fu rong you cui', in which a lot of famous actors and actress of Sichuan opera work for it, will be performed in K... Stage every night. Some of Sichuan opera stunt, such as Clown (Rolling Lamp), Spraying fire, Changing faces will be shown in it. We hope you will enjoy it.*

The show was good and varied – although if there had been any more of the opera singing, I would have had to leave. I enjoyed the small ensemble's playing, where the *erhu* took the solo. This instrument is sometimes referred to as the Chinese two-stringed fiddle, and it can produce some amazing sounds. There were also comedians, fire-eaters, jugglers who used both hands and feet, shadow and stick puppeteers, and best of all, the mask dancers. I am still in awe of the way that they could flick their masks so fast, colours and decorations changing with the blink of an eye. It was scary and rather eerie. The presenter of each act spoke in Chinese and English, the latter at quite a speed so that it was hard to catch what she was saying. When there were spoken parts in the acts, the English translation was displayed on two small rectangular screens either side of the stage, so low that you could choose to either watch them or the actors. Sometimes the screens showed the same words; at other times, you had to look at the left one and then the right, like reading a book, except the pages were miles apart. I only discovered that by accident. After a while, I decided to concentrate on the acting and forget the words. The translations were so strange that I could have spent my time laughing at them, and not the original humour. I was surprised, and annoyed, when on three occasions, three different mobile phones, belonging to Chinese members of the audience, started ringing. The first one I thought was part of the comedy act, but the next two dispelled that conjecture.

The following morning, we returned to our local café for breakfast, and it was then that I had one of my meltdowns. Piped music was filling the air, too loud for comfort, and western – hopefully not for our benefit. At some point, I became aware that I knew the song, 'To Where You Are', sung by Josh Groban, and as the chorus resounded, I knew that this trip around, I was the one doing the singing.

> *If only for a while to know you're there*
> *A breath away's not far to where you are*
> —Josh Groban

The tears flowed, and I choked up. It became a public moment, but I should have got myself to a safe corner, out of sight and dealt with my emotions on my own. Maybe it's just as well I live in a quiet, little town where I can do just that – on most occasions.

We took a bus to the Pandas. That word just has to have a capital letter because I doubt there is anyone on the planet who doesn't find their faces appealing. In spite of this, for those of you who only have the toy variety, mostly the white is not white, but a murky beige colour, whether natural or from lack of washing, I'm not sure. That was such a disappointment, although in some of the many photos we took, some of the pandas look as though their heads are frosted with fresh snow.

Our visit to The Chengdu Giant Panda Breeding and Research

Centre proved to be a good day out. First of all, we ventured into the museum and shop, although no one bought any souvenirs or gifts until the end of our visit. On returning to the open air, my gaze landed on a large black notice board covered in white lettering, western style. 'What's all this about?' I wondered as I read, 'Chengdu Municipal Rules Pertaining to Civilized Tour' at the top. That was followed with this exhortation and some regulations: *In order to build a civilized and harmonious tour environment and to improve the moral standards of both tourists and our citizens, please abide the following rules:*

1. Don't spit. Don't spit the chewing gum.
2. Keep silent. Don't jump the queue. — Please do not talk loudly in public places.
3. Don't pick flowers — or beat animal.
4. Don't climb up the historical relics. No photos without permit.
5. Do not be out for small advantages. Save water and electricity. Don't waste food.
6. Don't force foreign tourists to take photos. — Respect religious customs of different nationalities.
7. To be polite. Wear clean and proper clothes. Do not wear clothes exposing the neck or shoulders in public places. — Do not utter dirty words.
8. Advocate a happy and healthy way of life. Resist super-stition. Avoid pornography, gambling and drug.

Chengdu Municipal Spiritual Civilization Office

2006, November

There was a lot more than that, but I have quoted some of the rules that intrigued me the most, and I tried, at the time, to imagine such a notice displayed at the entrance of the London or Helsinki Zoos.

The weather was cool, and sometimes there was a slight

drizzle in the air – just as well, otherwise we might have exposed our necks – and the pandas loved it. Giles and Yoshi had been here the previous summer, and the pandas had been out of the sun, and out of view. Today they were hungry and more than willing to show us their feeding habits as they ripped up bamboo branches and proceeded to strip them for eating. They seemed to have plenty of space to move around in with grass, trees, and rocks in abundance. There were many other visitors, both foreign and native, but not so many that it felt uncomfortable.

One large lake we arrived at was teaming with goldfish, not like the ones that swam around in a bowl in my childhood home, but large varieties mottled with shades of gold, black, and white. We had just had some lunch, and we must have been feeling frivolous because we asked some passers-by to take some photos of our group. Someone had the idea to all stand with our backs to the lake and squat; that had become a favourite word amongst the females of our party. So squat we did, and I was laughing so much, I wet myself. I've checked the photos though, and you can't tell. I was dreading that there was going to be a puddle underneath me on the wooden boards. Well, I was squatting.

During our several-hour visit, I can vouch for my party that no one poked a panda, or avoided walking under a ladder, having been warned by the Civilization Office to resist superstition. None of us plucked a pack of cards out of our pocket and started showering a table with notes bearing Mao's head, nor did we have any saucy pictures concealed on our persons as far as I know. What would have happened if we had done any of those things, or any of the others that were forbidden?

In the afternoon, on our return to the city, we went shopping and sensibly decided to break into two groups – men and women. We had no idea where we were going, but ventured into a market area as well as a vast department store selling everything. We had to drag Jane out of the shoe section, or she might still be there. Up and down escalators we went, stopping to look at various items, until we finally found the jewellery. The others wanted to buy me a thank-you present for helping to arrange the trip, and although I didn't need something tangible to feel their gratitude, it does make me a little nostalgic to have the earrings and necklace that I now wear with pride.

Finding our way back to where we had arranged to meet the men, we realised we had some time on our hands – and there was Starbucks. My only knowledge about these coffee houses was what I had gleaned from the press, including my weekly *TIME* magazine, and I must admit that I have never read any of those articles to the end. This chain has not made it to Finland in spite of the fact that Finns drink the most coffee per capita in the world according to some statistics that I found – more than four times the consumption of the UK and more than double that of America. The others knew the ropes, so I let them get on with it.

Before we had finished our fare, we spied the men congregating outside, and their looks said, 'We might have guessed that's where you would all be.' During their shopping spree, they had bought a watch for Giles, also in gratitude for all the hours and energy he had spent, and was still spending, to ensure a smooth ride.

We crossed the main thoroughfare and tried, unsuccessfully, to hail some taxis. Giles said he was going to walk, and we all decided to do the same and stretch our legs. Our group soon straggled out along a busy road lined with small shops. The last part of the journey took us alongside a canal with the reflections of fairy lights dancing on the rippling surface.

Adjoined to our breakfast café was a Thai restaurant, so rather than go back to our rooms, we went straight there for our last meal together as a group of ten. The food was delicious, and I loved the way it was presented, especially one rice mixture in half scooped-out pineapples.

Alfred, Ben, Giles, and I had the earliest flight in the morning, and I was thinking that we would say our goodbyes before bed, but the British contingent had decided to come with us and wait at the airport rather than in the hotel. Everyone was bleary-eyed, but we managed to load the two minibuses with luggage and bodies and retrieve the correct bags at the airport. There was a mix-up about when the later-flight members should book-in, but in the end, we all got through security. The four of us went ahead to find our gate, and I had to dash to the toilet because the strange diet had finally caught up with me. It could also have been because I knew that the main part of our adventure had been accomplished, and I felt I could have made it smoother by not allowing my personal feelings to cloud my demeanour. Exiting from the loo, I found the rest saying their goodbyes to Alfred and the boys, and I did the rounds, not knowing what to say and letting my hugs speak for me.

I spent the flight listening to my sons talking about education, one home-schooling his daughter, and the other currently a maths teacher in a fee-paying school, wanting to join in, but failing to find the courage to express my opinion, too afraid of being shot down in flames, I suppose. Their sparring was deliberate though and gave me topics to think about.

A leaflet that I had picked up in the hotel added some poetic relief, as I read a headline, *Drunk in Green – Green Attraction*. Intrigued, I continued reading. '*I like water of D—, closest to mother's breast milk. The water spread in this mountain, city, forest and dam little by little after being wrapped with vigor green in billowy, or loquacious, or flamboyant, or elegant manner in the front, back, left or right.*' I felt disappointed that we had not been able to visit. It sounded interesting.

Having arrived in Shanghai, we went to the maglev train station where Alfred, Giles, and I would be continuing our journey within the city. There, we said our goodbyes to Ben, whose flight to London left in a few hours from the same airport.

'Goodbye, Ben.' Did he catch, 'I love you'?

Chapter 17

Farewells

There and Back

The washing from before our trip had dried on the clothes-horse in the living room, and after Giles left to play his weekly football game, I folded and replaced it with the load that he had put in soon after our arrival back in the flat. Alfred and I watched *BBC World*, then he had a nap, and I tried to catch my breath.

So many thoughts were racing around my head, and I knew that I hadn't been able to talk to the boys in any way that my pre-trip thoughts had anticipated. Their dialogues hadn't needed to include me, so my self-imposed refusal to try and join in wasn't noticed.

On his return, Giles cooked us a meal, and we chatted, Alfred still reminiscing about earlier days. I prepared for a day alone with him the next day when Giles would be in school. I was using the master bedroom that night as Alfred was now in the guest room, and Giles would be watching an Everton game into the wee hours in the living room. I snuggled down with a book and fell into a fitful sleep. I was already awake when I heard Giles come for his shower in the adjoining room, but I didn't say a word. The flat door clicked, and he was gone – the professional back about his business.

Alfred didn't want to go out, so we stayed in the flat, silently reading, watching the news, and him telling me about his family in Australia. He produced a bundle of photos of his grown-up children, grandchildren, and his Chinese wife and wrote neatly on the backs of some of them to give me.

I had been planning, from the day we knew that he would be back in Shanghai with us and not staying on in Lanping, to take him to the sushi bar for this Monday's lunch. The day before, in what context I don't recall, he had said that he had read that sushi was unhealthy. That was quite a broad statement, as sushi rolls can be filled with a vast array of ingredients, but that put the lid on my outing. I found some vegetables in the fridge, chopped them up, and made a soup. A bit of spicy paste that I also discovered made it better, and all of the soup disappeared. I had been thinking there might be some left for Giles when he came back from school, but we polished it off.

Yoshi arrived back from Sri Lanka, and the four of us went to a Japanese restaurant for my last evening. That night I slept in the living room on the couch that Giles had been on the night before. It felt a bit like musical beds. After the others had retired, I finished my packing and checked, again, that my passport, self-printed ticket, and money were all in my small bag and readily accessible when needed. As I shut my case and strapped it tight, I decided that my nightdress and last minute things could go in my small backpack in the morning.

Knowing by now that mornings were not conducive to chatter, I didn't attempt to engage Giles in conversation as he readied himself for another day at school. I made my coffee and sat on the sofa bed, notebook in hand. 'Expectations (can only?) lead to disappointment.' 'Dad did *not* build banisters for bunnies!' The page became populated with my musings and queries. The day before, Alfred had told me that he had given all his ancient photos of China to his son Martin, so 'Are there any dates on Martin's photos?' became an issue that might settle the discrepancies about the livestock. Looking at Giles through the corner of my eye, I wrote, 'So much to say, but no words with which to say it.' 'Caring and wanting to help do *not* equal fussing.' Now he knows what I was doing before he got up from the sofa, put on his coat, and gave me a hug goodbye. I hope he also heard my final words.

Alfred and Yoshi were coming to the airport with me, leaving in plenty of time for me to catch my ten o'clock flight home. The cleaner was due, but was not answering her phone. Consequently, she wouldn't know where to find the key. As we came out of the block of flats and were walking towards the taxi, she arrived on her bicycle, and her face lit up as Giles's elderly relative began speaking to her in Chinese.

My brother was delighted by the maglev ride, but I was already thinking about check-in, security, and what kind of travelling companion I might have for the nine-hour flight. 'Please, don't let it be somebody who needs to talk all the time,' I was thinking. Check-in was quiet; hence, I was processed at the business-class desk – a first for me. More hugs, and I was suddenly on my own. Tears welled in my eyes. I doubted if I would see Alfred again, and I was not sure when I could make another trip east, although in a few months Giles and Yoshi would be in Singapore, which might be a new destination to try. It was a long walk to the gate, which I found first and then backtracked to spend the few remaining notes I had in my purse, paying ten times more than I knew the goods were worth in this economy, which I tried not to think about as they were the normal price in mine. The only ladies' toilet I could find in the vicinity had a door that couldn't be closed, let alone locked, but I put my backpack in front of it and hoped for the best. This was China after all.

Returning to the waiting area I heard through the garbled amplifier system, that my flight was not embarking yet, even though the scheduled time had passed. I sat and waited for the message that would say that it *was* time. Getting nervous now, I got up and went to check what was happening and found that people were going down the escalator. Finnish-looking people. I followed them, hoping for the best. There was still a queue for boarding, so I wasn't late, but I did wonder what message all the people already sitting comfortably in their seats had heard through the loudspeaker. By the time the plane rose into the sky, we were an hour behind schedule, which suited me fine. I would have one hour less wait at our destination.

No one joined me in the double seats; that was neat, being able to spread my feet, not have to wake someone up, ask them to put up their table and move their shoes in order for me to go to the toilet, and no one checking what movies I watched. What did I watch? A film with Meryl Streep – one of my favourite actors – and lambs in the title, but I couldn't tell you what it was about. Those little blue earpieces were uncomfortable, and as I tried to get them in the right place every five minutes, I lost a lot of sound.

The food was good and recognisably western, but with an oriental twist, and, as usual, I put unneeded wet wipes and toothpicks into my bag. About an hour from Helsinki, some passengers started getting agitated because they had connecting flights. It was at this point I realised that Helsinki must have become a main hub for China destinations as a list of places with departure gate numbers came up on our screens. The passengers were spreading out to so many places, all across Europe. I wondered how many would make it to their flights in time.

I disembarked in Helsinki airport in the early afternoon, Finnish time. Proceeding through passport control, after phoning home to say that I had arrived on Finnish soil, although I wouldn't be leaving the capital for another four hours, I walked the length of the domestic terminal and waited. I tried to read, but mostly I watched the people gathering for other flights and tried not to think about it being late evening for me. By the

time I had flown to Tampere, driven back in the car with Arto
and reached my, oh-so-wonderful bed, it was almost five o'clock
of the next morning for my Chinese clock.

Getting up at the normal time, I set about the washing, my
own and an accumulation from home. In the evening, I had one
of my Conversation Groups, and I still don't know how I managed to stay coherent.

The day before I left China, Giles had put the photos from all
the cameras onto a CD for me. I put it in the computer to see
how many there were, but the folders labelled John, Steve, and
Ruth were empty. Mike still had to send his to everybody, so I
asked him to include the rest. About a month passed before they
arrived in the post, and it was interesting to see what moments
others had caught through their lenses. I had already started
adding further chapters to my story about childhood losses, and
the photos jolted my memory and helped me relive the momentous adventure we had recently undertaken.

While looking through the hundreds of photos, I got the idea
to ask my fellow travellers if they would like to add some words
to this tale, to give another perspective. I also asked Harry's
grandchildren, the two who had been with us in China, and the
other ten who hadn't been, if they would like to share some of
their feelings when they heard that their parents were making
this pilgrimage and any reactions they had had on hearing the
results. Maybe I should also ask the three younger ones about
our first, pioneering trip.

I wonder who will decide to share their thoughts.

Chapter 18

Harry's Family Speaks

Reflections and Fulfilments

John (fourth child, second son)

It was an amazing time and wonderful to be with all the family. I was so surprised at all the changes in Lanping. Memories were very poignant – seeing where our mother and sister were buried, a place that is now a ploughed field. My bedroom in the house is still intact, and it was indescribable being able to view the Himalayan Mountains through those very windows, sixty-four years later, something that I had always hoped to be able to do again. Seeing them there made me realise how close we were to the Burmese border.

When Mr Li played hymns from long ago on his mouth organ, I remembered the Chinese words, and we sang together. Seeing him and remembering playing with him so many years before was very special. Many more memories came back, including being in church and hearing the town bell ring, which meant something official was happening in the square. I pushed my way through to the front of the crowd and saw a public beheading – I was only five! I also remembered our donkey having to be 'put down' after being bitten by a snake and American planes flying over to drop us supplies during the famine. On one occasion, I just managed to avoid being hit by tins of sweet milk falling from an unopened parachute.

I vividly remember the Americans flying us to Calcutta and a jeep coming to meet us at night. I was nearly seven and terrified, thinking it was a wild animal because its large 'eyes' were so far apart, and it was making such an awful noise. I remember knowing that a U-boat was following our ship for three days – so exciting for a small boy – and I also clearly remember the intense disappointment when the Red Sea turned out to be normal sea colour!

In 2008, the journey from Lijiang to Lanping took us about five and a half hours, while the one Dad and Mum made with Alfred and Ivy over seventy years earlier took twelve days on foot from the nearest road. On one particular occasion, on that very road, there were twenty-one mules, some coolies, and Paul Yang and John Hsieh, two Chinese evangelists who worked with Mum and Dad. All had gone well for the first eight days, but on the ninth day, they started going up the mountain at first light and on to the next stopping station, which was such a long way that darkness came while they were still a few hours away. The main party had gone far ahead as Mum and Ivy were being carried in a *hua-kan* by two coolies a lot of the way – like a stretcher that you can sit on. Dad got out the paraffin lamp to light up, but it was empty, and the paraffin was packed in the baskets on one of the donkeys far ahead. The Chinese started to unpack for the night on the mountainside, but Dad said they couldn't because of the cold and wild animals, so they were in a very difficult situation – a stalemate. Paul Yang then said, 'Elijah, in the Bible, stayed at a widow's house where the oil didn't run out until a famine was over. Hebrews 13:8 says, "Jesus is the same yesterday, today and forever."' Then Dad and Mum, Paul Yang, and Bawlor prayed. Dad tried lighting the lamp again, and it ignited. He then pumped it up, and it got very bright, so within the next few hours they got to the inn, and it was the Chinese coolies who told the rest what had happened! I have told this miracle to many groups of people and schools over the years and have seen a few miracles myself.

In 1944, when China was being invaded by the Japanese, we were in danger ourselves because we had been helping the Americans. Mum had died when I was three and a half; Dad had the five of us, and there was no way out of Lanping. During a meeting in our church, a young Chinese man of sixteen began praying and then started to speak in perfect English, which he didn't know a word of – just as it says in Acts 2:4. He said words to this effect: 'Trust me, do not worry any more. I will bring you out, and I will be with you.' Many hundreds of miles away, a Major Kaplan, who was in charge of transport in the 'Far East American Bases', was already arranging for a transport plane to come and land within a mile of our home, which it did, and it brought us out to Calcutta. We then travelled to Bombay, coming to England on the last British convoy through the Suez Canal, and on to our new home.

These are just a few of the things that I remember from my early childhood in China, and all of us have different stories to tell....

This trip to China has brought some of us back together again. In addition, it's also been great to get to know, and be with, Ben and Giles, my nephews. It's also been good for Ann, my wife, who originally didn't want to go, but who now can't stop talking about our trip. We feel truly privileged and grateful to God for the extraordinary experience. In view of what happened just a short time after getting home, the earthquake that shook part of the country and claimed so many lives, we can only pray now for this amazing country, which we have come to love very much. We will always remember arriving in Lanping and seeing this huge modern town side by side with the remains of our old home, which, incredibly, was still intact, but was due to be demolished just after we left.

We personally are also so very grateful to those who helped organise this incredibly special trip for us, and to my eldest brother Alfred for translating on so many occasions – it's an experience that we will never forget. Also to my other brother and sister who came with their spouses, who helped us share in this wonderful experience. This is also for our brother Paul and his wife Ruth, who were not able to come due to illness. A special blessing for all of you.

Faith (sixth child, third daughter)

I never imagined I would revisit China – so really it was deeper than having a dream. It's hard to describe the emotions I felt as they were so varied, extending from an overwhelming sense of loss to an incredible peace. Standing in Mr Li's courtyard, the area felt like home with the beautiful view and the mountains beyond. I was thankful again in a deeper way for such amazing parents who had left their homeland and families to pioneer a work in this remote part of China. Meeting some of the people of Lanping, you could understand how easy it was to love them. It was so good to share these experiences with my family – it's a time I will never forget.

Mike (husband of third daughter)

For my part, the trip to Lanping was truly amazing. I had an ambition to take Faith to China ever since we got married in 1967, but never really expected to achieve it, let alone to find the houses where Faith and her family had lived. The trip gave me a little insight into what it must have been like to be a missionary in Yunnan, albeit seventy years earlier than our visit. I started to realise the tremendous sacrifices they made and the courage they must have had. It was also great to be with so many of the family who were children of that missionary. I left China with a real love for the people, especially those in Lanping, whom I will always pray for.

Tamara (fifth child of fourth daughter)

I posed these questions – or we would still be waiting for some input – and they and the answers were written on paper.

Q: What did you think when I first told you about going to China?

A: Wow! ☺

Q: What did you feel about Lanping and finding the old house your grandfather had built?

A: Cool! ☺

Q: What was the best part of the trip?

A: The mountains and the little dog in Lanping and the Great Wall. All? ☺

Q: Anything else to add?

A: No! ☺

A girl of few words and many symbols, which were all different, but cannot be reproduced here.

Giles (second child of fourth daughter)

These words were written after he checked some of the facts about careers, computers, journeys, prices, rivers, schools, and towers for me, and my asking whether he had written his few sentences. Little did he realise that I would use his answer as his quote: 'I don't know what to put.... From what I've just read, I think I'm mentioned in it quite a lot – that's more than enough for me!'

Chapter 19

The Journey Continues

Searches and Discoveries

I thought I'd finished, and then it began again. After sending my final manuscript for a professional edit, and before my son, Thomas, had got my website to the stage where I could use it, I decided to try again to find anyone connected to the names in my father's notebook. I started with the first one from August 1942 and immediately found a match. Oliver Milton, known as Oscar, was mentioned in an article written by Khine Tun, a Burmese woman who had taken several China-Burma-India (CBI) veterans back to the areas where they had been stationed. I wrote to her asking if she was still in touch with him, but she told me that her most recent emails to him had been returned, but she would check with someone else.

Meanwhile, I had been looking through the loose letters folded in the notebook. One was handwritten, and I entered the signed name into the search engine and clicked on one of the results. There on the screen was an old black and white portrait with a signature scrawled across it, looking remarkably similar to the one I had just copied. Suddenly, I realised that the letter I was holding in my hand was not from an American serviceman, but from J. F. Rock, an Austrian-American who lived between 1884 and 1962 and who had been, among other things, a botanist, photographer, explorer, and ornithologist. According to my investigations, he had first gone to Lijiang in 1922, and this became his base for the next twenty-five years or more. Initially, he had been sent to south-east Asia in 1920 by the US Department of Agriculture to gather seeds from a tree that would later be used in medication for leprosy, but in 1923, the National Geographic Society had become his sponsor, and, as a photojournalist, he had produced nine articles, spanning the years from 1924 to 1935. It is thought that these writings inspired James Hilton to write *Lost Horizon* with its exotic location of Shangri-La, a book which had been very exciting for me as a teenager more than thirty years later, although I failed to register the fact that the places described were in the same area of China in which my father had lived. In more recent years, one town in Yunnan that felt it might have been the catalyst for the book has now officially renamed itself after Hilton's imaginary land.

As well as those activities, Rock collected and introduced to the US, various trees and plants, including nearly 500 species of rhododendrons. He even had his name given to a hardy peony that does well in Finland apparently, but sadly, is not the species growing in my garden. He also studied the languages of local peoples, including the Naxi, and spent many of his years in Yunnan collecting and translating thousands of volumes of their pictography.

Just weeks before finding Rock's letter, my pen pal, Tien Yung, had written in an email, in a different context, 'I remember I took a picture when I visited Joseph Francis Rock's former house several years ago at the foothills of the Jade Dragon Snow Mountains in Lijiang. The caption of the photo reads like this: Now it is a museum for travellers. During his expeditions throughout Lijiang, Rock wrote about his experiences for National Geographic. His bedroom is still kept intact on the 2nd floor. He enjoyed writing journals beside a warm fire there.'

At some point in Rock's expeditions further west in Yunnan, he had visited my father in Lanping. His handwritten letter is difficult to read, especially the name of the place from which he wrote and also the year in which he was doing so. From what I have recently discovered about his life, he could have been in that area any time from 1942 to 1944, so the last number of the date could be from any of those years, although he mentions a small child, so 1942 seems the most likely. The letter had been folded in two and then in three, the top sixth reading, 'Mr Fisher', with a flourish of an underline. The remaining area of the back of the letter had been used for mathematical purposes, and is covered in pencilled additions and divisions, but whether they were calculated while my father was still in China or later, there is no way of telling. I doubt if Harry ever realised that he had met, and received a letter from, a famous personage.

```
Weu Hua Ts'ien
Oct 22/42
Dear Mr. Fisher
     The weather is cold and nasty and I am having
a miserable time in the village living in an open
temple with food running short. I wished I had
given up the idea of going altogether. Your ani-
mals are better off than I am. I want to thank you
for your courtesy and further loan of the animals —
they are going back well fed. Kind regards to your
good self, to Misses Cook, Brown and Hewitt.
     Very sincerely yours,
     (sig.) J. F. Rock
     (double flourish underline)
     P.S. Hope the small child is better.
     Oct. 23/d
     Apparently plane delayed owing to weather condi-
tions, here raining, cold and uncomfortable. Again
many thanks.
```

It seems that Rock may have had a higher opinion of my father than other missionaries he had encountered in China according to what he wrote in a handwritten, unpublished article called 'Missionaries in West China'. The content seems to span many years, and he is very disparaging about those who cut themselves off from local society and seemed to put themselves above others, as can be seen from the following paragraph.

> I looked for signs of her mission, – till my eyes fell on a sign which read in Chinese Ye-su t'ang or Jesus Hall. In the doorway stood a huge, middle aged woman, who could be none other than Mrs. Marston. I got off my horse and approached the lady hat in hand saying "have I the pleasure of speaking to Mrs. Marston?" Whereupon the "lady" put both her hands to her waist and in a most patronising manner said: "Are you a Christian and what's your business". I felt shocked at such a reception, put on my hat and left the "lady".

However, he also had a sense of humour.

> Before the missionaries had returned to Likiang in 1927 I had come back to explore the Konaling and Minyag Konka Ranges, and one day there came a lonely missionary woman on her way to Batang, then an abandoned mission station. As there was no mission to take her in she came to me and asked if she could stay a few days. When my servants called me to the gate I beheld an elderly lady with a wash basin on her head for a hat and a little bundle by her side. She was the type that lived off the country and had apparently no church at home supporting her. I took her in and when Friday came along I said Mrs. G. if you have any washing to be done, to-day is our wash day and my boy's wife will wash your clothe, as men don't wash women's

```
clothe. I nearly burst with laughter when she rep-
lied: "Oh no I need no washing done. I wear black
underwear."
```

I continued checking the numerous Internet pages that had appeared at the mention of Rock's name and found a photo essay of when a journalist, called Michael, had retraced his footsteps in China. Where possible, he had also put the explorer's old photos of the same scenes he had photographed, and it was fascinating to see the two worlds, one above the other. I found an email address for him and wrote, explaining who I was, and asking why he had an interest in Rock. He replied very quickly and mentioned several books he had about the Hump and that part of the world. Maybe I'll have time to buy and read them – soon.

⁓

Trying not to get myself too confused, I entered some more names in the search engine, and, thanks to some Americans passing on their names to their sons, I found two identical matches. It always feels strange to write an email, or a letter, to a complete stranger, especially in these cases where I need to explain quite a bit of background before I can get to the point. There is always a fear in the back of my mind that the recipient will give up before they get to the crunch line – but these two didn't. Three minutes later there was a reply to the message I had left on a 'contact us' form for legal services, although I had stated that this was a personal request, saying that the person I was searching for was his father and asking for the name of mine. I replied with as much detail as I thought would be needed and got the following answer. 'I spoke to my father after receiving your first email and he remembers pretty much everything about his stay with your father and the children'.

Mr Marshall knew my telephone number from the form I

had filled in and had passed it on to his father, whose number he
now gave to me. I replied:

> This is really amazing! I have been 'searching'
> for my father most of my life, and to find someone
> who knew him in the environment that he obviously
> loved is wonderful. I don't think that your father
> or I should start phoning from the US to and from
> Finland, especially as mine is a mobile, but if you
> could ask him to tell you, or write down, what he
> remembers, I would be really grateful. I've just
> attached the last photo taken of our family, months
> before my father died in 1960. The five children at
> the back would have been aged two to thirteen when
> your father stayed with them.

I was so thrilled. This was the first person I had found from
the notebook who I could write to. I told his son about this
book and asked if he thought his father would allow me to use
his words. There was no electronic connection between them,
so whatever the father wrote would have to come by post or via
the son's email.

The next day I continued my search with fresh hope that I
could find someone else. In the afternoon, a reply arrived from
the other junior I had written to, and I learnt that I had found
the right son, the author, Joseph Freda, but that his father had
already passed away in 2003 and had been buried with military
honours in Arlington National Cemetery. He wrote, 'I will look
through my father's diary for any mention of missionaries. If
you'll give me your father's name, I'll keep an eye out for it.'
I replied with my thanks, attached a scan of the page where
his father's name, Matthew Joseph Freda appeared, and gave
him some more details about Harry. Matthew's name had been
written with an initial M. – if it had been in full, it's possible I
would never have found his son.

I would now have to wait. I was exhausted emotionally when my mobile phone rang in the evening, and a number, not a name, came up on the tiny screen, so I had no idea who was calling, although I noticed straight away that it wasn't from Finland or Britain. An American voice asked something – initially I hadn't got used to the accent, so I had no idea what the question was – but I soon realised who must be calling. Townsell Marshall Sr., the father of the lawyer, told me that it had been such a shock to get a call from his son the day before, to say that a daughter of Mr Fisher had contacted him, as he had often wondered what had happened to the family who had taken care of him and his fellow survivor, Aldo Cereghino, following an eleven-day trek through unknown and hostile territory, during which time they had not met a single soul who spoke English. They had stayed with my father from 8 to 16 December 1943, and on their departure, the local magistrate had provided them with two horses and six carriers for their journey to Tali, these days written as Dali, via Chien Ch'uan. Those latter details I knew from the notebook, but I hadn't known what their situation had been before their arrival, nor that Dad had had to kill one of his cows in order to feed the family and their visitors. My new American friend, who had been twenty-three at the time, remembered Alfred's name and asked how the beautiful little girl had fared, as she had been unable to walk because of rickets, presumably due to a lack in her diet. He was referring to Faith who had been two and a half at the time of his stay. He asked me to tell all the 'children' that they had often been on his mind and said that he had something to send me. I came off the phone, and I was shaking – my first verbal contact with a person who had known Dad in China, and whom Dad had been able to help to health and safety. Again it made me wonder about the timing of events – the fact that I had not had the notebook and old photos before my first trip and had been unable to find anyone from the notebook before the second one. Why was I finding people now?

The next morning, I was writing another email to Burma to thank Khine for her interesting email about her life, which had included some time in London when her late father had been an attaché at the Burmese Embassy, when I received one from her. I was so sad to read that she had just heard from Ken Joyce, her friend in Australia, that Oscar had passed away two months earlier at the age of ninety-two. Ken hadn't known Oscar personally, but he had found his phone number and spoken to his widow. I hadn't realised that Oscar had been living down under, nor that he was English and had been with the Forestry Commission in Burma extracting teak at the time of the invasion there. This information quite surprised me as Oscar had been a major when he was with Dad, and had been accompanied by two captains and a lieutenant and his wife. One of them had written the following entry, which I sent to Ken for his perusal.

> Speaking on behalf of the above party I would like my thanks and gratefulness for kindness received from Mr Fisher to be recorded. We were the 'saddest' bunch of human specimens you ever saw, suffering from malaria, dysentery, exposure and exhaustion. We had marched from Fort Hertz in North Burma on extremely short rations. Mr Fisher took us in, fed, bathed, sheltered and attended to all our wants. I will never forget his kindness and also that of all members of his household.

I expressed my surprise to Ken that a teak worker would have been a major. The next day, although days were becoming mixed-up by now as I was holding 'conversations' with several people east and west, he sent me the following reply.

> It is no surprise to me that Oscar would have been commissioned in the Army. At the time he would have been aged 26, whilst the bulk of the people in

```
the forces would have been aged 18 to 20. (I was 19
when the war ended!) The fact that he was a Major
so close to the start of the Japanese war probably
meant that he had been in the Army Reserve prior
to the invasion of Burma.
```

૯૭

My previous day had continued with me entering names into boxes and pressing go. I read through many pages and wrote down some names and postal addresses that *might* be of children or relatives of the men I was interested in. I found another name on a genealogy site and I wrote an email to the contact person, asking if she was related to the person I was seeking. I learnt that she wasn't a relative, but that Aldo Cereghino had died, his widow lived in Oregon, and I could check for an address on www.whitepages.com. Not knowing what this was, I did as directed and found myself on a person-finder site. I entered what little information I had and found an entry with the right surname. Thinking this might be a son, I wrote a letter to him by snail mail. Meanwhile I checked the ancestry site again and discovered that the serviceman would have been a young teenager at the time he was in Lanping if the date given for his birth was correct. I passed on my observation to the woman who had so kindly helped me on my way through the maze, and was told that after she had investigated further, she had ascertained that the birth year should have been entered as ten years earlier. She also told me that she had just found some more information, including the fact that Aldo Cereghino, his wife, and three children, had flown from Scotland to New York in 1954. What had they been doing on my birth island when I was three years old?

When I got to Chaplain Vernon O. Rogers, whose message to my family is quoted in chapter ten, I was surprised to find a letter written to him from Martin Luther King Jr. in November 1955, thanking him for preaching to his congregation during his absence on a speaking trip. I can't be sure that this is the same minister who had one of my siblings harnessed to him in case of an emergency, but I would like to think so.

Captain Audrey E. Rogers's name was on the next page of the notebook, and she had this to say: 'We have certainly enjoyed having the Fisher Family stay with us on their way through. We are very grateful to them for their help of downed crews over the Hump. May they have a safe journey home.' I discovered that as chief nurse working under Major Morris Kaplan, she had become the first American woman in Burma to earn the Purple Heart, following being wounded in the calf of her left leg by bomb fragments while loading a plane.

I decided to try searching for Major Kaplan again. His was the only name that had ever meant anything to me, presumably because of his visit to us in England in 1960. I clicked on one of the items and watched a *CBI Roundup* page appear from December 1944. This had been a weekly newspaper published between September 1942 and April 1946; over half of the issues are now available online, not merely scanned, but recreated using modern technology to make easier reading, by Carl Weidenburner, the son of a veteran. I typed 'Kaplan' in the 'find' box for that particular page, and the text jumped down and showed his name highlighted in green at the bottom of the screen. My eyes travelled upwards and were caught by the caption under a half-hidden photograph in the top left-hand corner.

THE REV. HARRY G. FISHER & BROOD
Helped 17 Americans Lost In Jungle

I couldn't believe my eyes. Here it was at last – what I had always thought would be there, but had never been able to find. Here it was. The black-and-white photo showed a middle-aged man and his five children huddled together, all looking lost and bewildered. They were watching something happening on their left, apart from three-year-old Faith, the youngest, who was looking directly at the camera, maybe wondering what other new experiences were waiting around the corner. I could hardly read the article through my misted-up glasses.

ATC [Air Transport Command] PAYS DEBT TO BENEFACTOR OF HUMP JUMPERS

CALCUTTA — The ATC has repaid, in some small measure, a debt to a notable benefactor of its Hump fliers. Recently flown from China to Calcutta, and then safely seen aboard a plane bound for Bombay whence they were to travel to their home in England, were the Rev. Harry G. Fisher, British field worker of the Tibetan Border Mission and his five children.

Fisher, stationed for the past 16 years in the Lan Ping District of western Yunnan, during the past year provided food, clothing, shelter and medical care for 17 Americans who have later "walked out," and buried seven who were killed. In addition, his efforts have given the Search and Rescue Squadron of the ATC's India-China Division, and companion organizations, invaluable information and insight with respect to the mysteries of this wild terrain.

On Nov. 23, 1943, the first four wandering ATC bailouts found their way to the Fishers' home for a 10-day stay which was to start them to their base and to safety. The visits of subsequent distressed airmen varied from four days to 20.

The Rev. Mr. Fisher never would accept anything in repayment of his kindness. He asked only whether it would be possible to drop some canned foods to replenish his larder, and some extra blankets in order to take better care of future visitors.

Among Fisher's American guests was a non-flier, Lt. Robert Wesselhoeft, Jr., stricken with infantile paralysis, while on a photo-mapping expedition.

Unable to breathe, Wesselhoeft was kept alive 14 days at the Fisher mission by artificial respiration, and then flown out in an L-5 whose pilot, Maj. Welch, worked the lever of a primitive lung-compressing apparatus with one hand and flew the little plane with the other for three hours. Wesselhoeft was later taken by ATC to Calcutta in a hospital plane and after more than two months in a hospital, was flown to Washington in an improvised iron lung, stopping at the Azores to pick up Lt. Mary E. Hoadley, a flight nurse who had once attended Fred Snite, Jr., in his iron lung in Miami. Lt. Wesselhoeft arrived in Washington sufficiently recovered from his ordeal to joke with reporters.

Several months ago Capt. Rolland Bennett, an ATC officer, visited the Fishers to coordinate search and rescue activities with them. Among the articles he carried into the jungle with him was an assortment of toys for the children. Bennett remained there two weeks, and during his visit learned that Fisher was under doctor's orders to leave the high altitudes of the area. On returning to his base, Bennett arranged air transportation to India. First came a six-day journey for the family through the desolate mountains, accomplished by mule train, and then a motor jaunt to the nearest air base. It developed that the two youngest children had never before seen a horse-drawn vehicle, let alone a motorcar. On arrival at the military establishment, they beheld their first electric light.

Crossing The Hump, the three youngest were each in the care of an American, in case of the necessity of a jump. Alfred and Ivy, the oldest, were instructed to jump alone but with static lines to open their chutes automatically.

Mr. Fisher is going home to England for good now. All their possessions remaining at the mission have been sold. The five children are his greatest care, their mother having died.

The Fishers took with them more than one tangible
evidence of American gratitude, among them the
shoes worn by the children on the trip. Shoes are
not easily obtained in the Yunnan wilds, and Maj.
Morris Kaplan, commanding officer of an American
medical air evacuation unit and one of the Fishers'
close American friends, heard that some were needed
at the mission. He requested the children's gra-
duated foot sizes, had five pairs of shoes made
and dropped them next time he flew over the lonely
settlement.

I wrote to Carl asking for permission to use the article, and
whether he had the original copy of the newspaper from which
he had typed the Internet version. In his reply, he told me that
he had obtained his copy from an online auction site, and,
according to his files, the page had been added in December
2007, which explained why I had not been able to find it earlier
in that year. He asked if my family would like to dedicate that
page to my father, and I am so happy that the last words there
now read, 'This page is dedicated in memory of Rev. Harry G.
Fisher.'

Three days after my initial contact with Joseph Freda, I
received another email in which he told me more about his
father.

My father kept a journal of his entire stay in
the CBI theatre, dating from June 12, 1943, to
January 24, 1944. Unfortunately, the period between
November 14 and December 11, 1943, is missing. My
father's plane was shot down on November 5. He
and the crew hiked along the Salween River until
November 15, trying to attract the attention of
a rescue plane by spreading out their parachute

panels to spell HELP - to no avail. They faced a
decision: continue on the easier trek along the
Salween but venture closer to Japanese-held territory, or scale the 17,000-foot mountain range and
enter the Mekong River valley, where there were
known missionary stations. Despite their fatigue
and injuries (they had worn through their boots,
and their feet were bleeding), they decided to
cross the mountains. The effort was considerable,
given their condition, and the altitude. It took
five days to cross over and enter the Mekong Valley.
A rescue plane spotted them on November 20. It
dropped badly needed supplies and a map.

Joseph continued his email by quoting from two publications
that further clarified information that I had found elsewhere,
which had sounded as though it was connected to my family,
but not quite. One excerpt was from a book called *Flying the
Hump: In Original World War II Color,* and had been narrated
by the pilot of Freda's group, Ted Carmack. Unfortunately, his
memory hadn't been as good as his rescue.

He spoke about a Miss Huett from New Zealand, who was
looking after three American children because their parents had
been unable to return to China owing to the war. According
to him, his party stayed for a day and were well taken care of,
and they shared some of the rations that the rescue plane had
dropped for them with their hosts. It sounds as though the children had never seen food in a tin before or tasted cheese, as Miss
Huett explained to the airmen that the youngsters had been
born in China.

Then Joseph made this comment, which I wholly agreed with:
'I think narrator Carmack got the nationality of the children and
their parents wrong – they were not American, but British —.'
He then quoted some paragraphs from an article called 'Four

Walked Out', which had been written for the March 1950 issue
of *TRUE* magazine, by James H. Winchester.

In this article, the number and names of the men involved
corresponds with those in Harry's notebook – Lt. Ted R.
Carmack, Lt. M. Joseph Freda, Cpl. James K. King and Cpl.
Murel E. Sampson. It said that this party had suffered many
hardships after they had to bail out, before they made contact
with a fellow American, a missionary called A. B. Cooke, who
was travelling north to Tibet. Next they met a British missionary
– yes, my father – who is merely referred to as 'Fisher', and
his housekeeper, Mrs Hewitt, and his four children. Carmack
had remembered there being three, but neither writer had that
number correct. According to the text, King was amazed at
how the children spoke Chinese in preference to English, and
he didn't let them out of his sight, probably because he was
missing his own children very much. I have tried to find some
connection to him, but have failed so far.

The writer continues his tale by saying that the party recovered their health and stamina due to Mrs Hewitt's care, and that
a rescue plane that had kept track of them dropped badly-needed
footwear and a map showing a route to where the Burma Road
and the Mekong River intersected. There, a message told them,
they would be met by a rescue party.

My link with the past then put together what I had already
suspected.

    So, Ruth, triangulating the facts in your email
    and the two published pieces, it looks like your
    father and your siblings are those who helped my
    father and his crew. It is too late to thank your
    father, of course, but please convey my deepest
    gratitude to your siblings for the sustenance they
    gave my father. From what I know of his trek over
    the Himalayas, this encounter with your family
    came at an opportune time.

I felt such a glow as I read those words, that I had been able to link past and present for both our fathers.

I tried to find the whole article on the Internet, but the main story in that issue of *TRUE* had been about UFO sightings – 'Navy Scientist Confirms Flying Saucers' – so the rescue story didn't figure anywhere. Joseph told me in an email that the other inspiration for the month included, 'bowling techniques, spear fishing, and Easter clothing trends (wide-brimmed felt hats, wing-tips, and monogrammed cufflinks).'

He suggested trying to contact Miss Hewett's family for more information. She had been a spinster – the one that Mr Li thought might be my mother – and from what I can gather, the mother-substitute that my older siblings hoped would not become their permanent one. Her marital status seems to have caused some confusion and her name has been spelt in various ways in the preceding articles, but 'Hewett' is how my father wrote it in the photo albums. Interestingly enough, when Harry and Victoria, plus Miss Hewett and three other spinster ladies, sailed to China together, her name attracted another variation and was spelt on the passenger list as 'Hewlett'. I have no idea what happened to her after 1945, or even if she returned to England with Harry and the children. As soon as I had written that, I sent an email to Alfred's two daughters in Australia and asked them if they could find out any more about her. The next day Christine replied: 'Dad said that some other missionaries were trying to 'match make' her with Harry, who thought per-haps he should marry her for the sake of the children, but Dad and Ivy told him not to, unless he really loved her! Dad said she travelled back to England with them and then went back home – he wasn't sure where.'

Her home address on the ship's list was in Birmingham, so maybe she returned there. She was about forty-seven by then and had given the best years of her life to China, the last few to helping a father care for his five motherless children.

·᷐᷐᷏᷑·

The day after I had written to the two sons, I had found another possibility. The two names and a middle initial were on a company page, and with my 'nothing ventured, nothing gained' spirit in overdrive, I sent another email to an unknown person on the other side of the world. Three days later, I had to write the following apology: 'I have just been checking through the emails I sent last week to several people whose relatives' names may have been in my father's notebook, and noticed that your email address was repeated five times in the 'TO' field. I have no idea how that happened and would like to apologise for it. It was not intentional.' I had tried to imagine a string of messages, all coming from the same sender, and realised that the recipient had probably thought they were spam. I hoped that my apology would make him realise that it wasn't. A week later, as I was wondering whether to try snail mail for this connection, a reply appeared in my inbox. I had found the right family, but Kent told me that his father, Frederick C. Keish had passed away in 2002, and his brother, who had been named after their father, had also died. He continued:

> I would be happy to look for any information that would help you. Like many men that fought in that war, my father did not talk much about his experiences. He did say that he experienced things that he would rather forget. My mother is alive, and, between the two of us, I feel that we can reconstruct some of the events. He did talk, although infrequently, about his journey to safety after being shot down as he had to have a lot of help, due to his severe knee injury.

I replied immediately, attaching scans of the pages where his father's crew had written in the notebook and giving him some more information about my father. Not long after, he wrote, 'As it happens, my mother is digging through years of pictures and papers now, and I will have her keep an eye out for any information.'

As she was looking, so was I, and later I found a typed letter that had been sent to Keish in Lanping, stuck into my father's notebook.

```
HEADQUARTERS 308TH BOMBARDMENT GROUP (H) AAF
Office of the Commanding Officer
A.P.O. 627, c/o Postmaster
New York City, New York
18 January 1944.
Dear Keish,
     Your squadron is leaving with two (2) jeeps and
a trailer today or tomorrow, and will go along
the Burma Road, through Yunnanyi, to Wayao, on
the Mekong River, about sixty (60) miles south
of where you are at Lanping. They should be there
about Saturday, 22 January 1944. You are to orga-
nize a party as best you can to go down the river
or the valley trail to Wayao. A map and compass
are enclosed to aid you. Good luck! We are all glad
that you are alright.
     (sig.)  Larry
     L. P.  Martin
     1st Lt., Air Corps, Ass't. Adjutant.
```

The evening before, I had decided to write a proper letter to the Memorial Chapel where the widow of a Morris Kaplan had been taken care of after her death earlier in 2008. I wanted to ask them to pass my letter on to any of the relatives who had been mentioned in the obituary. It was another long shot, and, without an email address, more work, but I had to try. A similar letter went to a funeral home about a brother of the deceased. I had also found another of the names in an online hospice newsletter from 2004 because someone had made a donation in memory of a person with the same name as I was trying to trace. I wrote an email to a contact person mentioned in the newsletter, asking if my message could be forwarded to the donator. That was returned as undeliverable, so I tried another address from the same page, but that person had also stopped working in the hospice it seemed, so I wrote another letter to go by snail mail. I was certainly giving a number of people, unrelated to the task in hand, jobs to do.

⟨✤⟩

Then the promised packet arrived, and what a lot of interesting material and photos it contained. Mr Marshall Sr. included a recent photo of himself and his wife of sixty-two years in a newspaper clipping, and also one of him in Kunming from the summer of 1943, which had been taken several months before he had stayed with my father. His letter started, 'Dear Ruth – Forgive me for using your first name but after our telephone discussion I feel as if I know you.' I had felt the same way. He continued:

> When my son told me that he had an e-mail from you I was very surprised to say the least. I had thought often of your family and wondered what had happened to them. After I left Lanping I had no way of communicating with your father so I never knew when he left China.
>
> My companion and I arrived in Lanping on Dec. 8 1943. We had bailed out of our plane in the evening of Nov. 26 in the Upper Salween River Valley and had been on the trail for eleven days. Sgt. Cereghino and I were the survivors. Two of the four-man crew were killed in the evacuation of the plane. During

this eleven days we had not seen anyone that spoke English so we had never known where we were.

Our guides took us to the Magistrate in Lanping – not long after we arrived at his house, Miss Hewett arrived – she soon took us to the mission, and explained that your father had gone to sell his wedding silver since finances were bad at the mission. – Mr. Fisher arrived back in Lanping the next day. The magistrate invited Mr. Fisher, Miss Hewett and us to a banquet which included 6-8 of the village elders. Having had very little to eat for eleven days we probably ate too much and paid for it the next day.

Mr. Fisher had a fattened beef steer which he asked me to help him butcher. He particularly wanted me to kill it with my .45 automatic gun – which I did. Having been reared on a farm in Kentucky I had helped kill several animals. Miss Hewett was a very good cook so we ate very well.

In my official report I did not discuss the family, but I had great feelings towards them. I couldn't imagine why anyone would leave civilization to live in a place like Lanping. I asked Mr. Fisher about conversion to Christianity, and I remember him saying that the Magistrate had converted, but he didn't know if that would last, when he, Mr. Fisher, left Lanping.

I'm enclosing some reports from other crews who stayed at the mission to give you a feel of the kind of people your father befriended. My friends at the base in Yunnan-yi told me that they took supplies to the family for Christmas 1943.

Among the papers that Mr Marshall enclosed was an eleven-page typed report that he had written a month after his bailout and adventure.

[It was] considered to be one of the most thorough

and valuable accounts of its kind in all our history as a Hump flying outfit. What Lt. Marshall and
his Radio Operator, [I have since learned that this
should have been 'flight engineer'] Sgt. Cereghino,
learned should prove of interest to the entire
command. This story calls attention once again to
the splendid and unselfish spirit of our friends on
the ground. They have been liberally rewarded with
gifts of food and other items unobtainable during
wartime where they live. Places and names of individuals figuring in this story have been deleted
out of consideration for security and safety and
possible future usefulness of these persons in our
search and rescue operations.

This was part of the introduction written by Capt. John
Nesbitt, whose letter to Harry, two months later, was quoted
earlier in the book in chapter ten.

Lt. Townsell Marshall's detailed report was a restricted document entitled 'Intelligence Bulletin #6'. On page eight are the
following paragraphs. The words in square brackets are my
additions.

The next day we went due North for about half
a day. Here the trail was very good. Soon we came
to quite a large village and were taken in to see
several Chinese. They had a map of China on the
wall. They showed us where we were. For the first
time since we had crashed, we knew where we were.
***** [Lanping]. After we had been there for half
an hour *****[Miss Hewett and who?] appeared. We
were very glad to see them as they were the first
white people that we had seen on the trip. After we
had explained what had happened and she had translated it for the Chinese Magistrate, she took us
to their home.

We were told that four other American flyers
[Carmack, Freda, King and Sampson] had spent eight

days there and had only left the week before. They
had sent a message to Yunnanyi ***** and the rescue
squadron had dropped them supplies and instructions
to go South *****. She didn't know which message
had gone through, but we sent a message asking for
clothing, food and medicine. The Magistrate sent a
runner back to the district where we had crashed
with orders to have the whole district searched
for additional survivors. This was December 8.

***** [Mr Fisher] arrived on the 9th and had the
Magistrate send a runner to ***** to send a radio
message to Yunnanyi from there. On the 13th the
rescue ship came out and dropped the supplies we
had asked for but gave us no instructions. The next
day, we saw the Magistrate and asked him for horses
and coolies to carry our supplies so we could leave
on the 15th; but he said that that was too short a
notice, so we had to postpone our departure.

On the 15th, the rescue ship was over once again
and dropped a message. We communicated with the
ship by spelling letters on the ground with our
parachutes. But still no instructions; ***** [Mr
Fisher] told us that there was a pretty good trail
over to ***** and that it would take us only six
days to make the trip. This seemed to be the surest
way to us; so we decided to go that way. Early on
the morning of the 16th two soldiers, five coolies
and two horses we left *****[Lanping]. The trail
was pretty good and we were able to ride about
half of the time. About dusk we arrived at *****
where we cooked our own food. The next day we went
through particularly bad robber country, so we had
a six soldier escort. The trail was still fairly
good.

The next pages continue with their trip to safety, and their
final arrival in Jorhat, Assam, on Christmas Eve. 'After an x-ray
had been taken of Sgt. Cereghino's ankle, it was found that it had

been fractured when he hit the ground. He also had an infection where we had taped his ankle. But in spite of those injuries, he had walked most of the distance that we had travelled.'

I kept wondering whether the letter I had written to a Mark Cereghino in Oregon, had found its way to Sgt. Cereghino's relatives.

I phoned Mr Marshall in the evening, at about the same time as he had phoned me, to make sure I didn't wake him up. I thanked him for all the fascinating material he had sent and asked him why he had reports from two people. He told me that several years previously a fellow veteran had been planning to write a book about the rescue efforts in the CBI arena, and had been collecting reminiscences. Unfortunately, that book never made it to printed form.

One was a seven-page handwritten account from Charles R. Kock, who had been with Harry from 15 to 20 January 1944. Realising that Frederick Keish had also been in that crew, I asked his son if he would like me to scan and send a copy of what his father had also experienced.

```
     That would be great. I talked to my mother and
she is looking for some letters your father wrote
to mine in the late 1950s.—She does remember my
father talking about your father and how there was
a baby there with a severe case of the rickets.
When he got back to the squadron, they started
dropping formula to your father for the baby. He
did talk to my mother often about his help and
how he would not have made it out alive without
his intervention. His knee was shattered and he
had several broken ribs and a dislocated shoulder
from the plane hitting him when he bailed out. He
was alone as his crew had bailed out much earlier.
Before he was finally out, he was being carried by
some locals that were also "angels" for him. I hope
we can find some more information on your father
```

as I would not be here if not for his bravery in helping my father.

It felt very strange – an Englishwoman sitting in her tiny office in a small Finnish town, uniting past and present Americans. Kock began his account by saying that he had been the navigator on a B-24 stationed at Chengkung, about fifteen miles south of Kunming. He described in detail the purpose of the particular flight that would result in him meeting Harry. After their bail out, the five members of the crew reassembled. The pilot Keish was the last to be found, as he had pulled his knee out of joint when his parachute opened.

We met some guy who could speak a little English. He must have been the Mayor or Magistrate. He arranged to have 4 Chinese soldiers escort us. We didn't know where we were going. Just followed soldiers. After 3 days we came to Fishers place. What a surprise to meet someone who spoke English. He told us that so many had come through his place that a rescue plane (B-25) passed over every few days. He then spreads strips of cloth on ground and somehow signals them how many and who we are. They come back 2 or 3 days later and drop food (C rations) and a map showing us where to go.

I enquired from Mr Marshall, through his son, what 'C rations' were, and he gave such a clear description that I could almost see and taste the contents.

They are individually packaged, pre-cooked or prepared rations. A meal consisted of one M-unit and one B-unit, as well as an accessory pack. The M-unit was a canned entrée such as meat stew with vegetables, or meat and noodles, or pork and rice; the B-unit (bread & dessert) contained hard

tack crackers, sugar tablets, energy tablets, and
packets of beverage mix; the accessory pack contained sugar tablets, cigarettes, sheets of toilet
paper, weatherproof matches, wooden spoon, and
such.

Kock continued his account:

While we were at Fishers, I went to town with
him to buy food. He bought pork, vegetables, and
rice.

Now, when we flew we had a survival belt with
money, a ten cent compass, and silk maps of India
and China. We would stuff extra money and dry socks
into belt in case we needed them. So, while shopping with Mr. Fisher I told him to buy a bigger
piece of pork because we have 5 more guys to feed.
I offered to pay for this, but he didn't want me to
pay. I could see he was running out of money and
food. So we came back with a lot more food. He was
so overwhelmed with our help.

I left my parachute there so his housekeeper
could make some clothes for the kids. His wife died
a few years ago and is buried in the back yard.
Between the 5 of us, we had about 80,000 Chinese
yuan, which we left on the mantle over the fire-
place. Since he wouldn't accept it, we told his
son where it was, and to tell his father after we
left. We stayed at the Fishers' place five days,
then started down the trail. The pilot had to ride
on a burro [donkey or beast of burden], because he
couldn't walk. This was the tough part. We hiked
about 9 or 10 days down along a small stream just
east of the Mekong. We were met at the Burma Road
by 3 or 4 jeeps. They took us about a day and a half
to an air strip where we flew back to Chengkung.

In your last letter you mentioned this Gruber-
Jones group staying 14 days at Fisher's place.

```
They must have eaten him out of house and home.
You also mentioned the Fisher children: I don't
know anything more about them, I thought there
were 4. I remember they were in desperate need
of clothes. After we returned to our squadron, we
told the Commanding Officer about these people, and
collected some old clothes and shoes which were
dropped to them by the rescue plane.
```

In the meantime, I had found another name from Kock's crew in an online newsletter from July 2008, which had listed people in their organisation having birthdays that month. I found an email address, and asked the recipient to pass on my message to the 'name'. It had included a middle initial, which always gives me a little more confidence that I've found the right person. About two weeks later I received a reply from his son Alan, and discovered that Lamar C. Cartwright was eighty-eight years old and in good health. He had been the radio operator for the crew where Frederick Keish had been the pilot. I phoned Mr Cartwright one evening, morning for him, and found him sitting on the back porch expecting a very hot day. He told me many stories about his time flying over the Himalayas and his later military career. On coming off the phone, I re-read Kock's words, and felt in a fresh way so much gratitude for the help that American forces had been able to give my family.

The other story that Mr Marshall had sent was a copy of a hand-written diary from the Jones mentioned in Kock's account. I discovered form Harry's notebook he was 2nd Lt. Craig M. Jones, a co-pilot on the 'Cornhusker'. While reading many web pages about this arena of the Second World War, I had found that the aircraft were often given names. Jones's entry for 21 January 1944:

```
Departed La chi ching at 9:30 for Lanping over
the mountains above the snow line, using women
```

```
carriers, who were slow. Arrived Lanping 5:30 p.m.
- beautiful scenery. Mr. Harry G. Fisher met us. He
was a short, dark-haired Englishman, with a black
moustache and no front teeth. 5 children, wife
died May 1943 [June 1941], children Alfred, Ivy,
John, Paul, Faith, and, Miss Hewitt.
```

The next day his story continued: 'Very nice house – bath tub etc. Took first bath – soaked my swollen foot. All signed short snorters. Wrote in their book that was for people (crews) who had stopped there. We were the only one with all members, and well.'

On 23rd he wrote, 'Swollen foot down, less pain. Children sang grace. Weather may close in till spring (Apr).'

He then copied all the information from the previous pages of the notebook, finishing with their own. Two days later, 'Put out chutes again. Weather looks bad. Played *Lexicon*. Visitors from Magistrate's came to invite us to dinner next day bring silverware.' Did he mean that they had been requested to bring their own cutlery? Typing the word *Lexicon* suddenly brought memories flooding back. This was – and still is – a word card game first produced in the 1930s, and I can remember playing it as a child. I wonder if it was the same set of cards that Gruber, Marlatt, Pfund and Jones had played with. Where is it now?

These various snippets about Harry and the children's lives gave me a lot to think about, and after a restless night, I checked some old photos of Dad where he was standing next to people. I had always thought of him as tall, having forgotten that I only knew him when I was a child. During those wakeful hours, I had been wondering if my memories were wrong. However, seeing him standing between Major Kaplan and another American just before he died, I didn't think he was particularly short as he was only a few inches below them. Maybe in comparison Jones was a tall man, or Harry had the weight of the world on his shoulders at that time. In the few photos there are of him in China, he is not smiling, and I wonder whether that was because he had no front teeth. When I typed that part yesterday, I remembered that he had false teeth, but I had never stopped to consider what state his mouth had been in before he procured them.

On my first visit to Lanping, there had been an old bath propped outside the door of the old house, and we had speculated whether that had been Harry's. Jones's words seemed to confirm that it was. How on earth had they managed to get that shipped and 'muled' in?

Jones's notes continued with an entry for 26 January. 'Rained most of day. 4:15 to Magistrate's for dinner. 5 pm Dinner. Left 6 pm.' The next day, the notes end on a negative note. 'Up at 8 am, breakfast at 8:30. Weather looks better. Put out parachute strips at 10:30. No planes.'

According to the notebook, they didn't leave Lanping until 7 February. At the end of their two-and-a-half week stay, they left with four horses and four carriers.

In the article about the first American group to arrive in Lanping that had been published in TRUE magazine, an American missionary called Cooke had been mentioned. Another one, or was it the same one?, came up in Jones's diary. For 24 January he wrote, 'Said "Goodbye" to Mr. Cooke – he's leaving tomorrow for Tali to pick up his bride. We have to go south.' If it was the same one, he had been very busy, as previously he had been on his way to Tibet.

I decided to check through the notebook again and found right at the back, tucked in between the cover and last page, a Christmas card, the message of which I had previously forgotten to type into the transcript. It was from the Marlatt of this last crew.

Dec. 9, 1953
Los Angeles, Calif.
Dear Mr. Fisher,
    With this card I would like to extend my sincere
wishes for good health and happiness for you and
all your family. I often think of you during the
year and wonder how everyone is getting along. Even
"little" Faith must be quite a big girl now. It's
so hard to realize how fast the time has gone by
since our goodbyes to you when you passed through
Chabua, India on your way home in 1944. Does it
seem like nine years ago to you? — I'd like you
to know that it isn't only at Christmas time that
I think of you - your name still enters our conversations many times during the year. Above all
I want you to know that your great kindness will
never be forgotten. Best wishes for a pleasant and
happy 1954.
    Bob Marlatt and family

It started me wondering why only this one card had been
preserved, as it sounded as though they were sent annually. Also
Kent had said that his father had received letters from my father,
so presumably there had been others sent in the other direction.
A few months ago I destroyed many letters written to me over
the last twenty-five years from various people around the world.
I wonder if in fifty years any of my children will wish that I had
kept them, as I now wish those to my father had been stored.

I had already contacted a site called accident-report.com,
which had lists of servicemen who had been involved in acci-
dents in several arenas, and I chose one name, filled in a form,
and paid for the documentation to be sent to me. Much of the
material was illegible, but I could make out the following words
from Craig Jones's report of the bailout of his crew.

```
We had made it over the ridge into Mekong valley
with the altitude dropping steadily. I got on my
parachute and held wheel while the pilot put on
his. I then went back to help lighten the load. I
got to throw out 6 cases. The pilot rang the bell
- went forward and set auto pilot. Went back again
to help radio operator on with chute. Pilot rang
bell and said "bail out". The crew chief went first
with the radio operator behind. I waited to pick
up musset bag and then went back and bailed out.
I saw the plane crash before I hit the ground. It
exploded and burned.
```

It was interesting to read about what had happened before their arrival in Lanping.

Several weeks later I received a reply from Dorothy Cereghino, Aldo's widow. My letter *had* gone to her son and she had tried to email me, but her message had been returned as undeliverable. She gave me the following information. 'In 2006 a gentleman from Illinois wrote to Al wanting information to include in a book he is writing about missionaries helping airmen in the CBI theater. My husband died April 6, 2004. I sent this gentleman a copy of Al's obituary, the debriefing reports of Lt. Marshall and Sgt. Cereghino concerning the incident, and information about a spiral-bound compilation of the many, many planes and crews that went down in that theater.'

I then learnt why Scotland had been a taking-off point. 'Our family spent 1951–1954 in Kent, England, while my husband was stationed at Manston Air Base. We are hopeless Anglophiles.' Also in the letter she wrote, '—my family will be eternally grateful to your father for helping Al when he so needed it.' That was more music to my ears.

In a later email she wrote: 'I have asked my children what

they remember about talks they had with their father about the incident. We all have similar memories of his telling about the danger rescuers put themselves in by helping them and about the horses furnished so he could get out with the painful ankle injury.' She also gave me the name and contact details of the person who had been researching for the book she had already mentioned. The last paragraph of the letter he had sent had stated that he was especially interested in anything that her husband could remember about 'Harry Fisher and family, the English missionary at Lan Ping.'

My 'conversations' and searches are continuing, but I have to call a halt to the sharing of them in printed form. I will be posting any additional developments and intrigues on my website.

All these men that I have mentioned or quoted, as well as many others I have not yet made any connection with, played a part in helping my father and his children, and I hope that these printed words can repay in some small way, my family's gratitude for their support.

Epilogue
Autumn 2008

It has taken more than two years for me, Harry's seventh child and fourth daughter, to write this book, during which time I have done more than make two trips to the other side of the globe. These journeys and experiences have widened my view of the world and made me more convinced that there is no ultimate 'truth' waiting to be found or clung to, even though this whole adventure was to discover a man who fervently believed there was. I am grateful to him, and my mother, for the deep faith they displayed in their lives, but I have my doubts as to whether he would have been able to understand the choices I have made in my life. Indeed, I wonder about them myself sometimes. However, make them I did, and like each individual, I have had to live with the consequences, good and bad. I think that even the so-called bad experiences in life can provide people with an opportunity to take a good look at themselves, change, and grow.

Dad has always been a distant and cloudy memory for me, someone who haunted the shadowy places, the areas of my life that I couldn't reach. My younger brother and I were not taken to his funeral, the custom of the day perhaps, and were thus denied the most precious thing that we could have learned about life. Not seeing his coffin lowered into the ground, nor the hundreds of people who came to offer their farewells, we were deprived of an experience that would have been painful, but would also have given us a chance to say goodbye in our childish ways. I believe it would have also spared me several years of believing that Jesus would bring my father back to us. Seeing my mother dispose of my father's clothes, books, and effects was a shattering experience. We had little money, and I can remember wondering where we were going to find enough to replace those things when he returned. Slowly, the finality of his leaving sank in.

As children and teenagers, we didn't often visit his grave, but on the occasions we did, I would try to deal with my thoughts just as we dealt with the grass and weeds.

On 14 July 1988, at the age of thirty-seven, I was living in London and knew that my future probably lay in Finland, so I decided to pay a visit to my father's grave the following day, the twenty-eighth anniversary of his death. I took the train from London to my hometown, followed by a bus to the graveyard. It was sunny and bright as I walked through the old, unkempt resting-place of many of my hometown who had gone before. I stopped by two small graves that had fascinated me as a child and then walked on through the broken-down gate that led to the newest area, already old. I knew roughly where the flat marker covered in green marbled pebbles was situated, but it still took some finding, as it was overgrown and the birds had pecked at some of the lead lettering. My mother had rarely brought us here, and none of us had looked after the grave regularly – he's not here, he's in heaven, being the explanation. I felt rather strange. I weeded around the area, cleaned the words as best I could, and simply knelt and wept, not knowing that the next time I would be here, Mum's ashes would have joined her best friend and husband beneath the ground, and a new name and date would adorn the headstone.

Feeling rather foolish, I poured a small bottle of non-alcoholic ginger beer and the contents of a packet of salted fish snacks over the grave. I had never done anything like this before, but I had heard that in the east, families offer food to their ancestors, so I had decided to do so, just once. I chose the drink that Dad used to make at home and the food for our name, as well as a memory of helping him eat his fish on those enchanted returns from his preaching trips. Beneath the green pebbles, I also placed a small photo of Ben and Giles. The three most important male representatives of my life – all would be left here on English soil. I talked to him then – words of thanks for my life, regret that I had disowned him as my father and that I had been unable to make my marriage work, and asked him to keep an eye on his two grandsons who were now symbolically resting with him. Finally, I said that I wished I could know he knew that I had been here today to visit him. Even as I uttered those words, I knew that it was impossible. When had I felt him near since his final departure in my childhood?

I made my way back to the railway station on the bus and boarded the train back to London. It was quite full, but I found a seat on the aisle. On the four seats opposite were four middle-aged men who I soon realised had had a little too much to drink. Not wanting to make eye contact with any of them, I gently lowered my head on to the headrest and closed my eyes, letting thoughts of the day wash over me. Breaking into my reveries, I heard one of the men say that they should sing some songs from 1951 – the year of my birth. My ears pricked up. *I just wanted to see Daddy for the day*, were the words that assailed my senses. I had never heard the words or melody before, but I couldn't believe what I was hearing – a child missing her father and just wanting to be with him, even for a short time, just for a day? Was this my answer? Did he know about my pilgrimage? The next song left me with no doubts, although I found it rather bizarre that a teetotaller had only been able to find four drunks to convey his heart.

Ever since, I had been trying to find this song – the first one is still out there somewhere – and only discovered it during the summer of 2003, while I was in the midst of re-living, through writing, some of the horrors that had been my life. It was on a CD of music from 1950, sung by *The Mills Brothers*, and I found it, quite by chance, just hours before seeing a rainbow arched over a bridge as we crossed a lake on our journey home. Once there, I played the song – 'Daddy's Little Girl'. Tears rained down my cheeks.

> *You're the end of the rainbow, my pot of gold.*
> *You're Daddy's little girl, to have and hold.*
> —The Mills Brothers

I have not heard his voice for most of my life, but these days, especially after my two journeys to Lanping, and learning more about him from those who passed through his mission station there, I can feel his heart.

References

Songs from which a few lyrics were quoted, in order as used:

Anita Cochran, 'Daddy Can You See Me' from *Back to You* (Warner Bros. Records Inc. 1997).

Richard Marx: 'Right Here Waiting' from *Greatest Hits 1997*, (Capitol Records Inc.).

Josh Groban: 'To Where You Are' from *Josh Groban* (143 Records/Warner Bros. Records Inc. 2001).

The Mills Brothers, 'Daddy's Little Girl' from *Hits of 1950 Original Recordings* (HNH International Ltd., Naxos Nostalgia 2002).

I have been unable to trace the song with the line, *I just wanted to see Daddy for the day.*

Books and papers mentioned in text (not including those already credited at beginning of book):

Hymns of Praise No. 2, Hope Publishing Company, Chicago, 1931.

China Call, Leonard Bolton, Gospel Publishing House, Springfield, Missouri, 1984.

Lonely Planet series of travel books. www.lonelyplanet.com

Lost Horizon, James Hilton, Macmillan, 1933.

CBI Roundup, December 28 1944, http://cbi-theater.home.comcast.net.

Flying the Hump: In Original World War II Color, Jeff
Ethell & Don Downie, Motorbooks International, 2004
(softcover).

Four Walked Out, TRUE magazine, Fawcett Publications,
March 1950.

Come and visit
www.rainbowmeetslake.net

where you can see some photos of my father's days in China in the 1930s and 40s, as well as some from our trips in 2006 and 2008. There will also be links to the various sites mentioned in this book.

For Americans who are interested in the CBI Theatre of the Second World War, I will also post a few of the pages from my father's notebook, and a list of all the names that were written there, or who signed various pieces of correspondence.

I will add some photos of Finland – the beautiful, quiet country that I am blessed to live in, and I intend to update the pages regularly with articles and quotes.

Should you wish to buy further copies of this book for family and friends, there will be links to various booksellers.

Welcome to www.rainbowmeetslake.net

With my best wishes,
Ruth

Lightning Source UK Ltd.
Milton Keynes UK
UKOW030648260212

187958UK00009B/8/P